THE INVESTORS' HANDBOOK

First published 1994

British Library Cataloguing in Publication Data
A catalogue record for this book is available from the British Library.

ISBN 0 948035 04 8

Published by:
Rushmere Wynne Limited
P.O. Box 491, Leighton Buzzard
Bedfordshire LU7 7ZS
on behalf of ProShare (UK) Limited

Printed by:
Spottiswoode Ballantyne Printers Ltd.,
Colchester,
Essex CO2 8JT

Illustrations by David Simonds

FOREWORD

BY SIR JOHN HARVEY-JONES

Your decision to buy this book may well mean that you are one of many millions of people who over the last few years have purchased shares in government privatisation offers. Hopefully you will have gained a financial advantage from both the dividend income and the capital appreciation which have occurred in many of these offers.

It is, however, possible that the mysteries and jargon of the stockmarket may still be confusing to you, and this book is an attempt by ProShare to explain the opportunities available to you as an investor.

Of course, for the uninitiated, there are dangers and it is vital that you understand fully not only what the stockmarket offers but what the risks are. This book explains both fully. If you enjoy reading it and want to know more, why not invest in *The ProShare Guide to You and Your Stockbroker* which is a good way of understanding how to get top-class professional advice.

The book has been written by a highly-respected financial journalist who manages to explain stockmarket investment in plain English, without jargon and in a way that, I hope, will help you.

Deeper share ownership is something I fundamentally believe in and I would like to thank you for buying this book and wish you all the best in your future dealings on the stockmarket.

Sir John Harvey-Jones
President 1992/94,
ProShare (UK) Limited

THE INVESTORS' HANDBOOK

by

Maggie Drummond

PROSHARE

CONTENTS

INTRODUCTION

There are ten million shareholders in Britain – individuals who have invested part of their savings on the stockmarket. Some are able to buy and sell shares and follow the fortunes of their favourite companies with a kind of ease and knowledge that would be admired by the professionals.

Many, many more would love to be able to – if only they understood how. ProShare's *Investors' Handbook* is for them.

The stockmarket can be a baffling place. It has its own language, its own way of judging and reacting to economic trends, its own fads and fashions for particular shares, industries and personalities.

All this gives it a mystique that intrigues as well as bewilders those who are newcomers and want to join in for the first time.

If all of this makes you feel like an absolute beginner you are certainly not alone.

The number of private shareholders has more than doubled following the popular privatisation programme that started in the early 1980s.

Also, share schemes, which give employees a stake in the companies for which they work, have proved successful.

There are now generous tax incentives to encourage individuals to invest in the stockmarket through personal equity plans (PEPs).

Even if you do not yet hold shares directly, the chances are that your financial future is nonetheless closely linked to what happens on the stockmarket.

Unit trusts, for example, have long been popular with investors. If you have a personal or company pension scheme, or an equity-based savings plan with an insurance company, you will, one way or the other, have your savings tied up in the stockmarket.

These are collective forms of investment where the managers decide which shares, or other investments, to buy and sell. The private investor is nevertheless still faced with a baffling array of funds from which to choose.

There is no substitute for having a good working knowledge of the stockmarket when it comes to seeing your way through the sales patter and deciding what types of investments will be best for you.

The incentives to save for the future have never been stronger – investment in the stockmarket is now a crucial element in an individual's long-term financial planning.

But, it is probably the least understood. So this handbook takes you step by step through the maze. It aims to answer all your questions – plus some you may not have considered and to tell you all you need to know about the stockmarket and how to make the best of it.

When you have read all the way through, you will have the basic knowledge you need to set about stockmarket investment. You won't always get it right – no one does – not even the professionals. But if you apply your common sense and judgement and keep your personal objectives firmly in mind you will succeed. You will find the stockmarket is a fascinating place – developing a real interest in events will be a crucial element in your success. We hope this book helps you to enjoy investing. And good luck.

1

What are shares and why invest in them?

What is a share?

A share in a company is just that. Buying shares in High Tech Enterprises plc (HTE plc) makes you a part owner for as long as you have them. Originally, our mythical company would have been privately owned, probably by the entrepreneur who started the business. In order to raise capital for expansion, HTE plc shares are offered to investors through the Stock Exchange, essentially a market, where they can be bought and sold at a price that reflects supply and demand.

Why buy them?

Whether you buy them through a new issue like a privatisation, or acquire them in the "second-hand" (or secondary) market which is the main business of the Stock Exchange, the reasons for investing in the shares are the same. You believe HTE plc is a company that is going to prosper in the future. Its profits are going to grow over the years. The dividend payments it makes to shareholders out of its profits each year are going to rise so you look forward to an increasing income.

You also expect the share price to rise – reflecting the profits and dividend growth which should make the company, of which you are a part owner, more valuable.

Buying shares is the most direct way of investing in the long-term success of a business – or indeed of the economy.

Shares are risk capital.

Companies can raise money in a number of ways. They can go to the bank and ask for a loan. The bank will receive interest, take a charge on some of the company's assets as security and expect the loan to be repaid at the end of the agreed period. The bank does not get any direct benefit from the growth of the business. If profits fall, it does not affect its return. If the company fails, the bank, along with other creditors, has a claim on the assets. However, shareholders are last in the queue.

They will only receive some payment if the company has assets left after all other creditors have been paid. Shareholders' returns are not guaranteed. Company profits can fluctuate – so can the dividend out of which they are paid.

Most companies will try to maintain their dividend payments even in a recession. But a large fall in profits will usually mean a reduced dividend and a lower return for shareholders.

Share prices fluctuate as well – often in a way that baffles shareholders. There are almost as many theories as to why shares go up and down as there are shares – but here are some of the reasons:

- Good or bad news from the company;
- The expectation of good or bad news from the company;
- Take-over rumours;
- Change of management;
- Economic news and other external influences.

We will discuss the impact of these and other factors in more detail in later chapters – as well as the effect of economic trends on share prices. Anticipating share price and market movements, so getting your timing right, is one of the key elements of successful stockmarket investment – and one of the most interesting.

Shares are different from other more familiar types of investments.

While there are risks with shares, the potential for reward is higher. As an example, let us take the standard building society investment – one of the most popular ways to save money. You receive interest on your savings and the money is safe and easily accessible. Building society savings are and should be an important part of your financial planning – but not all of it.

What is happening to the value of your capital?

When interest rates are high, as they were in recent years, the return may keep pace with inflation – or perhaps even better it. But when interest rates are low you run the risk of the real value of your savings being eroded. There is little chance of your original capital growing to keep abreast of, or better, inflation.

While you can receive a good income from shares (we will discuss this later), one of their main attractions is providing a hedge against inflation. As the chart on page 17 shows, over the long term, investment in the stockmarket has proved one of the best ways of maintaining the real value of your capital – and of increasing it. Which is why it has a crucial part to play in your financial planning.

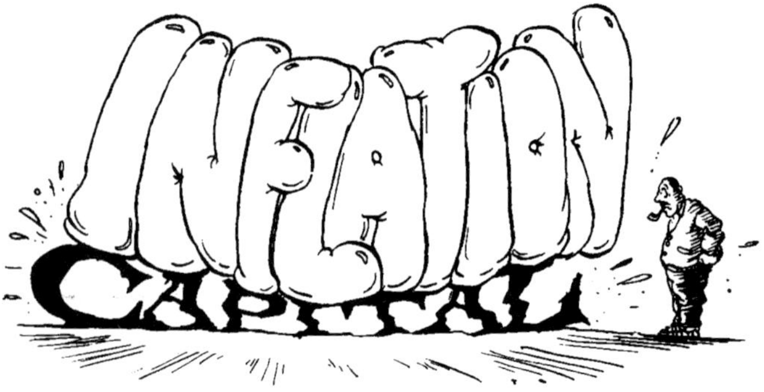

There are of course different kinds of strategies involved in stockmarket investment – and how you approach it depends on:

■ the amount you want to invest;
■ the time you are prepared to devote to it.

You might want to invest in "Blue Chip" companies – substantial corporations which are often household names, where a steady growth in dividends is the order of the day.

You might want to find exciting "high growth" companies, pin-point good recovery prospects, or speculate in "penny" shares.

We will deal with all these in later chapters and so help you decide what kind of share portfolio you should have.

But first, you have to look at your own financial position and decide how much of your money you should invest in the stockmarket.

Value of £1,000, in January of each year shown, if originally invested in January 1973.

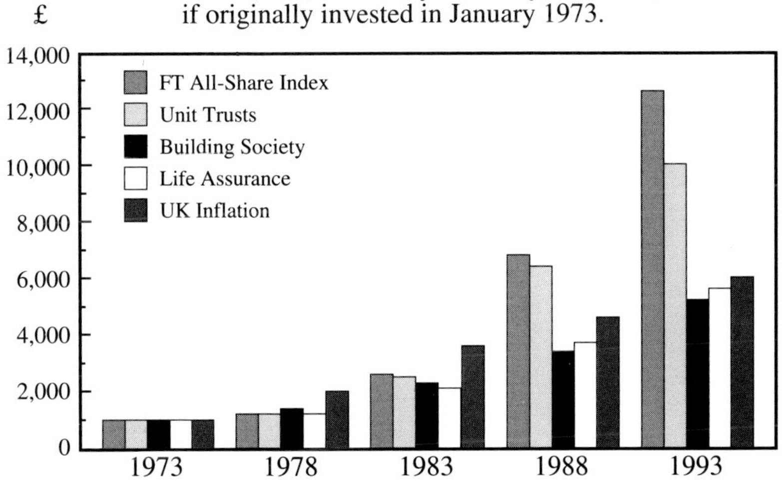

Figures supplied by Micropal Ltd, except UK Inflation supplied by BZW Research

2

Before you start.

Insurance.

If you have a job, a mortgage and a family, the most basic first step in financial planning is to make sure you have adequate insurance.

That means life insurance, mortgage insurance – maybe permanent health insurance as well.

What would happen if you were unable to work or you died?

Pension.

If you are in a company pension scheme you may wish to check your entitlements. If you have moved jobs several times, they may not look too wonderful.

Take advantage of the full tax relief available to top up – either by paying more into the company scheme by way of additional voluntary contributions (AVCs), or by investing in one of the many AVC schemes available from insurance companies.

If you do not have a company pension or if you are self-employed, you should put some money into a personal pension plan.

Short-term cash.

You should build up a fund of spare cash – money that you can put aside to earn a good return, perhaps in a bank or a building society: somewhere you can gain immediate access in a crisis.

What are you investing for?

No-one should have all their capital invested in shares – particularly if you are saving for specific items such as school fees where you are committed to spending at a certain point. A "with-profits savings plan" from an insurance company is one alternative – a tax-exempt special savings account (TESSA) is another.

Needless to say, buying shares is not the most appropriate way to save for a holiday, a deposit on a house, or a new car. What if your shares have fallen when you need the cash?

If you rely on your investments to produce a sizeable proportion of your income, you will need a high and predictable return from part of your portfolio – from gilts (government stocks), or guaranteed-income bonds for instance – or from higher-yielding shares.

Long-term goals.

Once you have decided on your immediate financial priorities, you can think about buying shares. The essence of share investment is to enable your capital to grow over the years.

For some people, the biggest concern is having enough

money to retire on comfortably – maybe retire early (this may not be voluntary these days), change careers, or just go fishing. Others want to leave a nest egg for their children.

To do all of these you need to make your money work for you.

In the next chapter, we take a closer look at the kind of shares you should be investing in and learn more about the workings of the stockmarket.

3

Types of shares, useful jargon and two key measurements.

There are 2,000 companies with share prices quoted on the Stock Exchange. Some are billion pound conglomerates – others are valued at just a few million. They represent the whole range of economic activity. Look at the daily list of share prices in the financial press. There you will find them divided into different sectors – motors, food retailers, chemicals, oils, property, and so on.

But how do you set about choosing which areas are for you?

Spreading the risk.

One fundamental rule of investment is to spread your risk – don't put all your eggs in one basket. That means building a balanced portfolio with holdings in several different companies

and industries. If one sector or company has a particularly bad time, you'll have your other shares to see you through. This doesn't mean, however, you have to stick only to big safe companies (they can have bad times too).

There should be some room for a bit of exciting speculation in your portfolio – it's fun and that's where you can make some real gains – or suffer some losses! But it's important to balance your wilder hunches with solid shares. You should work out what proportion of your money you should invest where.

Knowing your shares.

Unfortunately share prices do not come ready labelled "low risk", "high risk", "sure-fire winner", or "good old dependable". But the stockmarket recognises different kinds of shares – not just by size or industrial activity – as having particular characteristics. To build your portfolio you should get to know them.

Blue Chip companies.

These are big established companies – many of them are household names like Marks and Spencer, Unilever, ICI, British Telecom and Shell. They are the first division in financial terms with solid track records of substantial profits and dividends. They are large, valued by the stockmarket at over £5 billion – and form the backbone of the giant portfolios run by pension funds and insurance companies which need to buy and sell shares in large quantities. A lot is known about these companies – teams of stockbrokers' analysts spend their days researching them and producing regular reports. As a result, their share prices tend to be more stable than smaller companies, although there can be exceptions. Because of their size, they reflect the general movement of the economy, the stockmarket and of their particular sectors. They are a sensible foundation for any portfolio.

Growth companies.

Spotting one of these in its infancy – before it is generally recognised as something special – is every investor's dream. Typically a growth company will be in an expanding sector of the economy where a go-ahead management has produced higher-than-average profits growth for several years on the trot. It may have unique product or a technical edge. Anyone who

bought Body Shop as a new issue, or in its earlier years, for instance, will have seen a handsome return. Pharmaceuticals company Glaxo is another example.

These companies command a stockmarket premium – the dividend yield is lower and the price/earnings ratio is higher (see pages 29-30) because investors are buying the prospect of faster-growing profits and dividends for the foreseeable future. But this "glamour rating" is vulnerable if growth slows. Investors need to be alert.

Recovery shares.

Most companies reflect the general trend of the economy – but some shares really magnify the ups and downs. When times are tough, profits fall by more than average – but when things get better they can improve enormously. There are good profits to be made from these shares if you get the timing right. Industries like house building, car components, electronics and furniture retailing are where you will find plenty of recovery candidates, particularly as the economy comes out of recession – but check that the company is basically sound. Individual companies that have fallen on hard times for one reason or another can be good recovery prospects too – look out for a change in management for instance.

High-income shares.

Many consider high-income shares less risky than the glamorous growth shares, because when the opportunities for profits growth are poor, a good dividend yield means investors still get a decent return. High-income shares can give a good capital performance when the stockmarket rises as well, but you should choose carefully. A high yield can also be a distress signal – particularly one that is nearing double figures. It could well mean the shares are anticipating falling profits and a reduced dividend instead. You could be looking at a recovery share – or a company heading for the corporate graveyard.

Penny shares.

These are fun – offering you more shares for your money which makes you feel good. But be warned – they are a gamble.

A penny share only has to move by a few pence to produce a very large percentage rise – that's the great attraction – or fall, and that's the great risk. One drawback is that penny share "spreads" – the difference between the current buying and selling prices – can be disproportionately large. Some penny shares are companies where profits have fallen and might recover. Others may be "shells" where the business is stagnant. They are a target for entrepreneurs who see them as a backdoor way of getting a Stock Exchange quotation for their own business.

Anything can happen, and frequently does.

Useful share jargon.

Shares are sometimes described as defensive. This has nothing to do with jet fighters or tanks. It means that certain industries are less affected by downswings in the economy. Major food retailing companies for instance may be considered defensive – we all have to eat even in a recession.

Cyclical shares are the reverse of defensive – these are companies whose business and profits are very sensitive to economic trends – see recovery shares (page 26).

Highly-geared – sounds painful and can be. Highly-geared companies have large borrowings by comparison with their share capital. When interest rates rise, the increased cost of those borrowings can make a big dent in profits, magnifying the effect of any slowdown in the company's actual trading results.

Highly-rated – this can apply to a whole share sector where future prospects are considered to be particularly good – or to an individual company. The stockmarket puts a high value on these companies compared with the average.

Why not pick some individual shares for a hypothetical portfolio? Keep track of them for a few weeks. Watch how they respond to economic news, company news and the general trend of the stockmarket.

Later in this book we will take a detailed look at analysing individual companies. But you can't start to look at shares without understanding the two main yardsticks by which the stockmarket evaluates them.

Dividend yield.

A dividend is the amount of income paid per share each year to investors.

The dividend yield is the return from the income, expressed as a percentage of the money you paid for the share. In practice it is complicated to work out. Dividends are paid by companies with basic-rate tax already deducted but the yield is worked out on the gross amount – before tax is taken off. We will deal with the personal tax side later. For the moment you can look at the share tables in the financial press. Most show the dividend yield of each share listed. What are those yields telling us?

- A very high yield may be a sign that the company is expected to cut its dividend. The share price has already fallen in anticipation of reduced profits – but the yield is reflecting last year's pay out and not the lower amount expected.

- A low yield often indicates that a company's profits, and therefore dividends, are expected to grow faster than average. The share price has risen in anticipation of this rising income.
- Relative yields are a useful way of comparing shares. A company whose shares are yielding lower than the sector average may grow faster than one that is yielding higher than average.
- Yields on shares are the stockmarket equivalent of the rate of interest paid by other kinds of investments. Because the stockmarket offers the prospect of capital growth as well as an annual return, average dividend yields are lower than, say, the return from a building society, where the amount of the capital goes neither up – nor down.

Price/earnings ratio.

The price/earnings ratio is the stockmarket's other main tool for comparing one share with another. It tells you how many years it would take for the net profits after tax (known as earnings) to equal the current share price. We will explain earnings in more detail later. Assuming a company makes 10p a share earnings, and the share price is 100p, then the price/earnings ratio is 10 (100p dividend by 10p of earnings).

The price/earnings ratio is often simply called the "p/e" ratio. Sometimes people use the expression "so many times earnings", or "so many years' earnings". They all mean the same thing.

Many newspapers publish them in their share price lists. Once again, they can be misleading because they are calculated on last year's historic profits. Like dividends, they tell us different things.

- A high price/earnings ratio generally means that the company is expected to grow quickly, and increase earnings rapidly.
- A low price/earnings ratio effectively indicates that the company is rated a plodder, or one where profits might fall. Unlike dividend yields, price/earnings ratios cannot be compared with returns on other forms of investment.

4

Buying and selling shares.

Many investors get their first taste of the stockmarket through a privatisation or a new issue – the sale of shares in a company first "floating" on the market. You fill in the application form, send off the cheque and, if you are lucky, get the shares you want. Easy. But then what?

When it comes to buying more shares – or selling the ones you've got – many new investors are uncertain what to do next. You may want to back your own judgement from the start. You may want advice. Or you may want to find someone who will manage your financial affairs for you. Don't be put off by fears that no one is interested in the small investor. Many firms are – but to get the kind of service you want, you have to do a bit of research.

Where do you go next?

The main organisations that offer share buying services are stockbrokers – these firms are members of the London Stock Exchange and their main business is buying and selling shares for their clients. Some of the largest firms are market makers as well. They deal in shares on their own account, holding large quantities on their books and making prices according to supply and demand.

Others act just as stockbrokers – agents who buy and sell shares through the market makers on behalf of their clients. It is important to understand that one stockbroker can be very different from another when it comes to the services they offer.

Nowadays a stockbroking firm may be part of a huge financial conglomerate in the City. Or it may be an independent company specialising in private clients.

There are many good stockbrokers outside the City – and other firms who are mainly interested in institutional business from large investors. Before you approach a stockbroker, you should find out what kind of firm it is. A free directory of private client stockbrokers is issued by the Association of Private Client Investment Managers and Stockbrokers (112 Middlesex Street, London E1 7HY), which makes choosing a suitable stockbroker much easier for you. You may, however, choose to purchase *The ProShare Guide to You and Your Stockbroker*. This book gives a step-by-step guide to choosing a stockbroker. It costs £9.95 (£7.95 to ProShare Association members). See Chapter 17 for details.

Banks have been keen to advertise their services to small shareholders in recent years – you can now go into some branches and buy shares at the touch of a button. Many banks own stockbroking companies – even if yours does not, it will buy and sell shares through a stockbroker on your behalf.

Some building societies offer share dealing services. When there are privatisations the building societies often organise special facilities for investors.

You can buy and sell shares through independent financial advisers. They will not be members of the Stock Exchange but they will have to place your orders with a Stock Exchange member.

What kind of service do you need?

The Association of Private Client Investment Managers and Stockbrokers (APCIMS) Directory explains the range of services available. But before you choose a firm you have to decide what kind of service you want.

Dealing or Execution only.

This is the most basic buying and dealing share service for those who don't need advice or help with financial planning. Many private client stockbrokers offer this kind of low-cost service – taking orders by telephone or post. Most banks, some building societies and the specialist telephone services offer an execution-only service, as well as stockbrokers. If you are very confident of your own judgement – or only want to buy and sell shares very occasionally – an execution-only service could be the cheapest option. But it should be stressed that there is no personal contact – no on-going relationship – and investors are on their own when it comes to decision making.

Advisory.

But if you want someone to talk to and advise you on stockmarket investment you will find that most stockbrokers offer an advisory service for private clients who want to take the final decisions themselves. If you want to take an active interest in share investment without going it alone this might appeal to you. You may pay a little more but it gives you access to the firm's own research and investment ideas – and you get a sounding board for your own ideas. An advisory service is non-discretionary. This means that the final decisions are left up to you.

There are different kinds of advisory services – you may just want advice on specific shares – or you may want a stockbroker to keep tabs on your whole portfolio, providing regular valuations, for instance. Some stockbrokers stipulate a minimum size of investment before they take on a client. Others may want to establish how active an investor you are likely to be. When it comes to choosing a stockbroker there is no substitute for meeting the person who will be dealing with your account face to face and making sure that you both know what your personal investment objectives are. There are plenty of stockbrokers specialising in private client business – there may be one based in your locality.

Portfolio management.

Stockbrokers and independent financial advisers offer portfolio management services to private clients who prefer to hand over the prime responsibility for their investment decisions to professionals. Portfolio management is usually offered as a discretionary service. This means that once your investment objectives have been established, shares will be bought or sold on your behalf without your being consulted first – but you will be informed after each and every deal. You may need to have a certain size portfolio before you are taken on – a few firms may stipulate a minimum of £100,000 – others may try and steer clients with less than, say £50,000, into unit trusts instead of shares. But, as the APCIMS Directory shows, there are plenty of stockbrokers requiring £10,000 – or no minimum at all. A portfolio management service could include annual valuations, advice on tax planning, regular stockmarket information, administrative paperwork and safekeeping of share certificates. The cost of these may be covered by an annual charge or by separate fees.

Whatever service you opt for, make sure you understand the basis of charging and are absolutely clear whether it's discretionary or non-discretionary.

How much does it cost?

Stockbrokers make their living on the commission paid by clients when they buy and sell shares. Each firm will have its own rates based on the size of the bargain – the value of the shares bought and sold. There are no fixed rates, costs vary from firm to firm, and there will probably be a minimum charge for small deals. Intermediaries are entitled to add their own charge if they deal with a stockbroker on your behalf.

Many stockbrokers still charge between 1½% – 2% to purchase shares of up to £5,000 to £8,000 in value, reducing the percentage commission on a sliding scale for larger amounts. Smaller bargains may have a minimum charge – this could be between £15 to £35 or more. A larger minimum charge may suggest the stockbroker is not really interested in small investors – a lower minimum indicates the firm is keen. Other share dealing charges are ½% stamp duty (on purchases only) and sometimes a compliance charge (which helps pay for the regulators). Once the deal is done, you will receive a contract note which you should keep carefully. The one we reproduce on page 39 illustrates the total cost of buying a small parcel of shares.

At the moment the Stock Exchange trading calendar is divided into periods called accounts. These are two, sometimes three weeks long. If you buy or sell shares you pay the bill or get your cheque on settlement day – the Monday six days after the end of the account. This system will change in July 1994 when a rolling settlement system will be introduced. From then on all share deals will be paid for 10 days after the actual transaction. By the end of 1994, the period will be reduced to five days. This important change is the prelude to the introduction of CREST – a new electronic settlement system expected to be phased in over the next few years.

The commission charge is not the only thing to look at when

Specimen Contract Note

CONTRACT NOTE

NatWest Stockbrokers Limited

Member of the London Stock Exchange.
Member of the Securities and Futures Authority.
Member of the NatWest Life and NatWest Unit Trust Marketing Group.

55 Mansell Street
London E1 8AN
Tel: 071-895 5000
Telex: 883395
VAT Registration number 243 4890 53

MR & MRS A CLIENT

WE HAVE BOUGHT
FOR YOUR ACCOUNT AS AGENTS

KEY : CLIEN0001

Bargain Date & Tax Point 03 MAR 1994 for settlement 21 MAR 1994 804 @ 234 AA
Reference FFB00033 SECURITY 0565402

08:30 400	MARKS & SPENCER ORD 25P	419P	£1,676.00
	TRANSFER STAMP	£8.50	
(VAT NO RECOVERY)	COMMISSION MINIMUM	£35.00	
			£43.50
			£1,719.50

BARGAIN EFFECTED WITH SISTER COMPANY

MR & MRS A CLIENT
1000 HOP ALONG LANE
TIPTREE
HERTS

Please see over for bargain conditions | E. & O. E.

Subject to the Rules and Regulations of the London Stock Exchange. A member of the National Westminster Bank group. For the purposes of Value Added Tax and Capital Gains Tax it is recommended that this note be retained.

Registered Office: 55 Mansell Street, London E1 8AN. Number 1959470 deciding who to deal with. A good broker may get you a better price, which can more than make up for his higher charges. Some brokers cut charges because they do not carry out your order at once – and you may suffer for that delay.

Try to find out just how much attention you are going to get – a small country firm may be a better deal for the modest investor than a City one with lots of large clients and heavy overheads to cover.

Make sure you know the basis for charging right from the start – whether there is an annual charge for instance.

Even if you opt for the discretionary portfolio, keep an eye on what is going on. Make sure you are not being traded in and out frequently (know as "churning") and paying lots of commission to the broker, without much profit to you.

If your stockbroker is also a market maker, he should tell you when you are dealing in a share where his firm makes the market. That means he may be selling you shares his firm owns, or buying shares his firm wants itself. In some cases, this will mean you actually get a better deal. It should never mean that you get sold shares his firm wants to get rid of.

Beware of independent financial advisers who ring regularly with suggestions of shares for you to buy. They may have bought a lot of them cheaply, and be selling them on to you at a higher price.

Never buy shares in companies which are not listed on the London Stock Exchange, no matter how persuasive the salesman. They are far easier to buy than to sell and it may be extremely difficult to obtain a fair valuation.

5

What makes share prices move?

Whether you are sizing up an individual share or looking at the market as a whole, it's most important to grasp one fundamental point: successful stockmarket investment is about anticipation – assessing what is going to happen in six months, a year or even 18 months. Understanding that is as important as keeping an eye on what is happening at the moment. This is one of the things that baffles people about the stockmarket. When a company announces a big profits upturn it is often greeted with indifference by the stockmarket – the share price may even fall. This is because the profits increase was anticipated – the shares had already risen – to use the jargon, the upturn was already "in the price" – the market had already discounted the good results.

The professionals, the share analysts and fund managers, will already be looking a year ahead. Is the company going to produce another spectacular rise in profits? Will there be a slowdown in growth? Even more confusingly a share price may perk up after revealing poor profits or a loss. The thinking may be that the bad news is now out of the way, things are going to get better and now is the time to buy.

In Chapter Six we will be looking at how you analyse individual shares. But first it is important to understand what influences the broad trend of the stockmarket. You don't have to be an economist – you'll find it's largely commonsense.

Read the newspapers, particularly the financial press, on a regular basis and you will get a good idea of what people feel about the economy, where it is going, what are the underlying economic trends. All this influences the mood of the stockmarket.

When investors feel gloomy about the future, share prices tend to fall – this is what is known as a bear market. When they feel prospects are good or improving share prices tend to rise – this is a bull market. These phases can last for several years although individual shares can "buck the trend". And while it is certainly true that the stockmarket tends to amplify and exaggerate underlying trends, these movements are based on what investors believe is happening.

Interest rates are crucial as we have seen all too clearly over the last few years when the high cost of finance has resulted in huge numbers of company and personal bankruptcies and falling profits and dividends. High interest rates slow down the economy, discourage consumers from spending and hit profits. Low interest rates stimulate it as companies are encouraged to invest and expand and consumers take advantage of cheaper credit – all of which helps corporate profits. Although the impact of lower interest rates will take some time to work through, share prices will start to anticipate the upturn in corporate profits well in advance. This is the big picture.

Picking individual shares.

When it comes to picking individual shares it's clear that some companies will benefit more, and sooner, than others from falling interest rates. If consumer spending looks as if it should pick up, the high-street retailers will be among the first to benefit, as will companies with large borrowings (so long as they are basically sound) – or industries like house building that are particularly sensitive to interest rates.

The trend in interest rates is also important when it comes to deciding what kind of investments you should hold. When interest rates are high, fixed-interest investments like gilt-edged securities can look more attractive then shares. At a time when business and profits are going to be under pressure, a high fixed return looks a safe bet compared to the dividends on shares, which, as we have seen, reflect the trend in company profits. When interest rates show signs of falling, on the other hand, the prospect of rising dividends and capital growth as the economy is stimulated makes shares far more attractive to investors seeking the best returns.

Shares can provide a good hedge against inflation which

diminishes the real value of your returns from other investments (like building society deposit accounts) by eating away at your capital. Company profits and dividends can keep abreast of or better inflation, so preserving the real value of your cash as well as providing growth if the underlying economy is reasonably healthy.

But excessively high inflation is bad for the economy – and ultimately stockmarkets. Since the late 1970s and early 1980s when inflation was running at over 20% a year at one point, governments have become very conscious of the need to keep it under control. The main way they have done this is to put up interest rates and, as we have seen in recent years, that can bring the economy juddering to a halt with catastrophic results.

Exchange rates are an important part of the investment scenario as well. Many major companies earn a substantial part of their profits abroad, providing a hedge for investors against any fall in the value of sterling. Exchange rates also influence domestic economic policy. For instance, our first ill-fated attempt to join the Exchange Rate Mechanism (ERM) – designed to keep the EC currencies in line with each other – resulted in a long period of high interest rates as we struggled to keep the pound within the ERM. That was disastrous for UK business and, even if we re-enter the ERM, the lesson has hopefully been learned.

Devaluation of sterling, such as we experienced when we

came out of the ERM in autumn 1992, is a mixed blessing. It makes British goods cheaper abroad, providing an initial boost to exports. On the other hand it puts up the price of imported goods and raw materials – so it can be inflationary as well.

There are of course a host of other economic indicators that influence the stockmarket – and no two commentators will ever agree on the various implications.

Stockmarkets are sensitive to political and international events – the short term moves up and down can be alarming. The UK stockmarket is influenced by what happens on other stockmarkets too – witness the events of Black Monday in October 1987 when a huge fall on Wall Street on the previous Friday triggered off a similar collapse of share prices in London and other international stockmarkets.

But what investors should look at is the underlying trend. There is a mass of information published every day.

What's happening in the shops – are people buying? The retail sales statistics are published each month. What is business confidence like? The Confederation of British Industry publishes regular surveys telling us what UK companies are thinking. Of course these indicators lag behind events and you need to look ahead. But consider the simplest share investment rule of all. **Buy when things appear to be gloomy.** Think about selling or switching investments when everyone thinks the boom is going to last forever. It's easier said than done, of course, and few investors are brave or lucky enough to buy right at the bottom and sell right at the top. But it illustrates how to use the information you have got to anticipate what is going to happen longer term. And no one gets it right all of the time.

When you look at the share prices in the daily press you will see one price quoted. This is usually the middle market price at

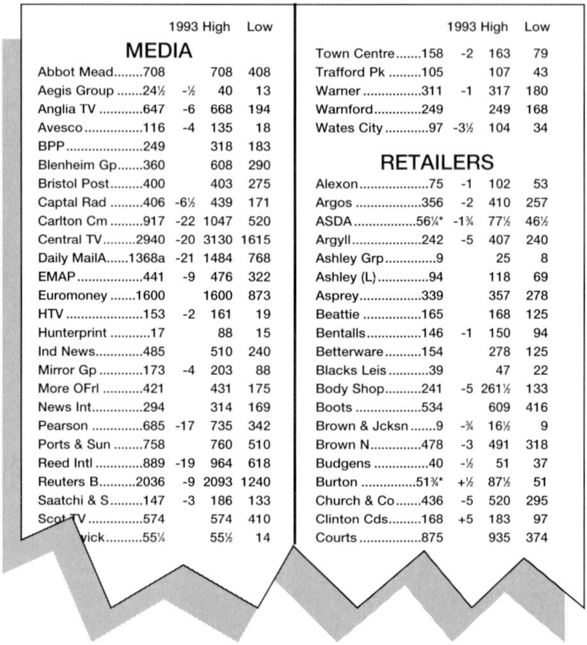

			1993 High	Low
MEDIA				
Abbot Mead	708		708	408
Aegis Group	24½	-½	40	13
Anglia TV	647	-6	668	194
Avesco	116	-4	135	18
BPP	249		318	183
Blenheim Gp	360		608	290
Bristol Post	400		403	275
Captal Rad	406	-6½	439	171
Carlton Cm	917	-22	1047	520
Central TV	2940	-20	3130	1615
Daily MailA	1368a	-21	1484	768
EMAP	441	-9	476	322
Euromoney	1600		1600	873
HTV	153	-2	161	19
Hunterprint	17		88	15
Ind News	485		510	240
Mirror Gp	173	-4	203	88
More OFrl	421		431	175
News Int	294		314	169
Pearson	685	-17	735	342
Ports & Sun	758		760	510
Reed Intl	889	-19	964	618
Reuters B	2036	-9	2093	1240
Saatchi & S	147	-3	186	133
Scot TV	574		574	410
[illegible]vick	55¼		55½	14
Town Centre	158	-2	163	79
Trafford Pk	105		107	43
Warner	311	-1	317	180
Warnford	249		249	168
Wates City	97	-3½	104	34
RETAILERS				
Alexon	75	-1	102	53
Argos	356	-2	410	257
ASDA	56¼*	-1¾	77½	46½
Argyll	242	-5	407	240
Ashley Grp	9		25	8
Ashley (L)	94		118	69
Asprey	339		357	278
Beattie	165		168	125
Bentalls	146	-1	150	94
Betterware	154		278	125
Blacks Leis	39		47	22
Body Shop	241	-5	261½	133
Boots	534		609	416
Brown & Jcksn	9	-¾	16½	9
Brown N	478	-3	491	318
Budgens	40	-½	51	37
Burton	51¾*	+½	87½	51
Church & Co	436	-5	520	295
Clinton Cds	168	+5	183	97
Courts	875		935	374

the close of business the previous working day. It is not the price at which you can actually buy or sell the shares.

When you buy shares, you pay what is known as the offer price which will be higher than the bid price that you will get if you sell them. The difference between the two prices is known as the spread. If you are buying shares in small or obscure companies you should check the size of the spread. If it's wider than average it could mean that the shares are not traded that frequently. When it comes to selling them you might find you get a poor price.

Share prices can change frequently during the course of the day depending on how many are being bought and sold through the market. When there are more sellers than buyers, the prices will go down. When there are more buyers, the market will move prices up. It's a question of supply and demand – the fundamental rule of any market.

When you place an order to buy or sell with your stockbroker he will give you the latest prices shown on SEAQ – the Stock Exchange Automated Quotations system. You should give him very clear instructions about the price at which you want him to deal.

"At best" means he will buy or sell at the best price he can at the moment of the deal – which, given minute by minute price changes, may differ a little from his original quote.

Your alternative is to set a limit on the price at which you want to buy or sell the shares. The stockbroker doesn't have to buy that day – he may allow you to leave the order for him to execute over the next few days if and when the price matches the limits you have given him.

Since your buying and selling will probably be conducted over the telephone you should ask your stockbroker to repeat the instructions just to make sure he understands what you want.

6

Looking at individual shares.

There is a mass of information available on individual companies whose shares are quoted on the stockmarket. Stockbrokers produce regular reports, the financial pages of newspapers comment on results, specialist publications like the *Investors' Chronicle* carry in-depth analyses. There are share tips (to be treated with caution) and profiles of company chairmen. All of these make good reading for the interested and help enormously when it comes to picking and following shares. But it is important to look at the information provided by the company itself to its shareholders.

You don't have to be an accountant to understand a balance

sheet or a half-yearly profit statement – and this information can be crucial if you are thinking of investing in a particular company. A non-shareholder can obtain the annual report and accounts from the company itself – write to the company secretary at the registered office – or maybe from the company's stockbroker.

Many company reports look like glossy magazines, so full of photographs that it gets confusing. Others may be quite austere. Whatever the presentation there are key features, common to all, that you should consider.

Profit and loss account.

This tells you how well (or badly) the company traded during the year – how much profit it made and how much dividend it is paying. This will be shown side by side with the results for the previous year so you can make a comparison. Most of the important information on profits will already have been included in the preliminary statement, which is normally made available a few weeks before the publication of the annual report and accounts. It is released to the Stock Exchange and the press, but not normally posted to shareholders. It gives the results for the year, but the annual report will give you a much fuller picture of what a company is doing.

Turnover means the amount of goods or services a company has sold. The annual report should disclose some interesting additional information – the proportion of sales overseas, for instance, and which divisions of the business are more important or achieved a better performance than others. You should look at the half-year interim results as well when you assess sales performance. Maybe sales slowed in the second half – maybe they are increasing faster. Obviously retailers do most of their business over Christmas and the New Year. The annual sales figure is not necessarily the whole picture.

Cost of sales and other expenses tell you how much a company has spent on running the business. It is a rough but useful guide to efficiency. If costs are rising in relation to sales, that could be a warning – or indicate an area that could improve with better management. This includes the major item of wage costs – though details will also be shown separately elsewhere in the accounts. It may also include depreciation, the amount set aside to cover the wear and tear on plant and machinery. In theory, depreciation builds up a fund to cover the cost of buying new machinery when it is needed.

The leading indicator of a company's performance.

Pre-tax profit is obviously a crucial figure – the one that is widely regarded as the leading indicator of a company's performance. But before that figure is struck the profit and loss account (see example on page 53) will show net interest which is worth looking at carefully. If a company has a lot of cash and few borrowings, net interest may well be a plus for profits. To assess the trading profit – how much a company is making from its actual business – you have to look at the operating profit. For most companies, net interest will be a charge against profits. For businesses with heavy borrowings, movements in interest rates are an important factor when it comes to assessing future profits. If interest costs are way up, it could mean the company has more borrowings and overdrafts – or that interest rates have been much higher.

These days, you are likely to find extraordinary or exceptional items next. Accounting rules are changing all the time. Extraordinary and exceptional items must be shown clearly in the profit and loss account. Old rules used to allow greater flexibility and leave scope for flattering profits.

Extraordinary and exceptional items cover unusual gains and losses made during the year. These might include profits from selling a factory or some other asset, the losses on closing a business and making redundancy payments, or the gain from selling a subsidiary company. Nowadays, the idea is that such items should be put into the profit and loss account where everyone can see them clearly, and understand what they mean. It will mean that profit records will become more erratic and the old idea of trying to present a smooth record of growth from continuing businesses comes to an end.

Tax.

Tax is the next major item. Net profits or profits after tax show you what the company made from its year's trading after all costs, charges and deductions. This is what the company earned. After deducting any preference dividends, this is the figure used to calculate the earnings per share we need to arrive at the price/earnings ratio – the important investment yardstick we described in Chapter Three.

Minority interests may figure next. These cover the profits

Typical Consolidated Profit and Loss Account

Profit and Loss Account (£000s)	Current year	Last year
Turnover	**150,000**	**100,000**
less		
Staff costs	(45,000)	(30,000)
Raw materials	(40,000)	(31,000)
Change in stocks and work in progress	(500)	(300)
Depreciation	(4,000)	(2,500)
Other external costs	(27,000)	(21,000)
equals		
Operating profit (before tax)	**33,500**	**15,200**
plus		
Net interest receivable	200	150
equals		
Pre-tax profit on ordinary activities	**33,700**	**15,350**
less		
Extraordinary items	(2,000)	(1,000)
equals		
Profit for the financial year	**31,700**	**14,350**
less		
Taxation	(10,650)	(5,160)
equals		
Profit after taxation	**21,050**	**9,190**
less		
Minority interests	(200)	(150)
equals		
Profit attributable to ordinary shareholders	**20,850**	**9,040**
less		
Dividends	(10,300)	(5,000)
equals		
Profit retained in the business	**10,550**	**4,040**
Earnings per share	**6.1**	**3.0**

or losses from businesses which the main company does not own completely, so part of the profit or loss belongs to an outside shareholder. If that business is making a profit, the minority interest will be a deduction from the main company's profit. If it is losing money, then the minority shareholder has to bear part of the loss, so the minority interest will show up as a plus in the main company's figures.

Some of the post-tax profit will be distributed as dividends to ordinary shareholders. The rest, shown as profit retained in the business at the bottom of the profit and loss account, will remain in the business and become part of the assets shown in the balance sheet, which is the next item in the annual report that investors should consider.

Balance sheet.

The balance sheet is not an infallible guide to a company's financial health. It shows what a company owns and owes on the last day of its financial year. You can be sure that it tries to look its best! Nonetheless, it is important to understand what the items in the balance sheet mean – how they can highlight a company's strengths and weaknesses. A specimen balance sheet is shown on page 56.

The first item is fixed assets – what the company owns in the way of land, property, factories, machinery etc. Theoretically the figure for fixed assets is what the company would receive if it were sold off. But the real value could be somewhat different, particularly if most of the assets are plant and machinery. It is worth looking at the valuation for properties. If they haven't been revalued for years they might be worth far more at present day values. Be careful. In the early 1990s, of course, values were falling. Properties valued in the late 1980s may look on the high side in later years.

Current assets include the company's stocks, cash, investments and money owed by debtors. The figure for stocks is very important – if that moves significantly out of line with sales you might wonder why. A big increase might suggest sales are not on target, or that the company has miscalculated demand – it might mean teething problems with a new distribution system. It costs the company money to hold stocks. It is always comforting to find plenty of cash or near cash in the balance sheet. As with the profit and loss account you can make a comparison with the previous year.

Current liabilities include the company's short-term borrowings – ones it has to pay back within a year – and money it owes suppliers and other creditors. High short-term borrowings might be a worry – particularly if the company's current assets do not include much cash. Running out of cash to pay the bills is how companies go bust, never mind how sound the assets may look.

After deducting these and other liabilities like long-term bank loans from the assets, the balance sheet gives a figure for net assets – what would theoretically be left to distribute to shareholders if the company sold everything and paid its debts. When stockmarket professionals talk about "asset backing",

Specimen Balance Sheet

Balance Sheet as at end of: **(£000s)**	Current year	Last year
Fixed assets		
Land and buildings	5,000	3,000
Plant and machinery	20,000	15,000
Total fixed assets	**25,000**	**18,000**
Current assets		
Cash at bank	2,000	2,000
Debtors	15,000	12,000
Stocks	12,500	10,000
Investments	5,000	4,000
less		
Current liabilities		
amounts due within one year	(14,000)	(12,000)
equals		
Net current assets	**20,500**	**16,000**
Total net assets	**45,500**	**34,000**
Shareholders' funds		
Capital and reserves	34,950	29,960
Retained profit (from profit and loss account)	10,550	4,040
	45,500	**34,000**

they mean how much these assets are worth per share. But as we have seen, it is important to study the balance sheet to see how the assets are made up and what they might really be worth. Clearly it is more interesting from the investment angle if much of the asset value lies in cash or near cash or very saleable land or property. It is not so exciting if it is all in ancient plant or machinery, which often may be worth less than it seems.

Watch out for gearing.

At the bottom of the balance sheet there is a figure for shareholders' funds. These comprise share capital and reserves, which are the undistributed profits of the business built up over the years. These are effectively the capital which finances the business. A key point to watch is the proportion of borrowings to shareholders' funds – known as "gearing" by the professionals. Acceptable gearing levels vary from business to business, but anything over 50% should be viewed carefully. It could mean a chunk of profits will be gobbled up by interest charges.

Much of the substance relating to the profit and loss account and the balance sheet will actually be in the notes to the accounts. It is important to read these carefully. Before you do, take a few minutes to wade through the statement of accounting policies. It may appear hard going. But as you become more accustomed to accounts, you will begin to see that this can sometimes be crucial. It effectively defines what the figures really mean. Pay extra attention to any change in accounting policies from the previous year. There will be a good reason for it – and do not necessarily assume that, if some phrase is missing one year, it has been left out by chance.

The annual accounts will also include a cash flow statement – this is an important part of share analysis. It shows you how cash has come into the business over the year – and what use has been made of it. Cash is generated mainly from trading profits – but there may be sales of assets as well, or new share issues. It will show how this cash was spent – on buying assets and paying tax and dividends. The point of this statement is to see if the company has a good cash flow (hopefully the amount of money coming in will match or exceed the amount going out). By looking at the changes in items like stocks and bank balances shown here you can learn a lot about the way a business is being run, whether it has sufficient working capital.

The auditor's report confirms that the annual accounts comply with the law and give shareholders a true and fair view of the state of the company. Sometimes, however, auditors' reports are qualified – usually because the auditors do not agree with some of the accounting methods used. But it is far more worrying when the auditors only sign the accounts on the understanding that the business is a going concern. That means that this company has financial difficulties and could go bust unless its bankers continue to support it.

The company will be well into its next financial year by the time the annual report and accounts is published so the chairman's statement may contain some information on current trading – and more may be revealed at the annual general meeting. Shareholders can go to that – and ask questions if they wish.

The report of the directors will give you information about any changes in company business or structure and will show the board members' own shareholdings in the company and the names of anyone else with more than 3%. It also tells you about any options the directors have been given to buy shares. That is a useful way of boosting their rewards from the company; a reasonable options policy can be good for both board and shareholders.

7

What's a share worth?

Open a copy of the *Financial Times* at the prices pages and there are hundreds of shares to choose from. Many other newspapers, too, also contain such financial information. Look more closely and each day there are some super winners and a few nasty losers. The key to successful investment is telling one from another. But before you can do that you need to be able to understand what all those columns of figures on the prices pages are telling you.

Vital statistics.

Pick any share. Going right to left across the columns you will find the previous day's middle market price (explained in Chapter Four). Then there is a column that shows you how the

price moved yesterday – by how much it was up or down.

Then it gives you the highs and lows for the year – you can see how much it has moved up and down over the last few months.

Next you will find the market capitalisation which shows the value the stockmarket puts on the whole company – the current share price multiplied by the number of shares in issue.

Then you have the dividend yield. This tells you the percentage return from the gross dividend declared on the shares at the present market price.

The final column shows the price/earnings ratio (usually referred to as the p/e ratio) the other important investment yardstick explained in Chapter Three.

Stockmarket sectors.

Whatever share you have picked will be grouped under a particular sector. If you look at the prices pages you will see a long list – textiles, property, hotels and leisure, food manufacturing etc. This is not to remind you that Marks and Spencer is a retailer. It helps you find the price you want more quickly. And grouping companies into sectors provides an important tool for comparing the share price performance of different companies. Next, turn to the stockmarket report page in the *Financial Times*. There you will find a table of the FT-SE actuaries share indices.

FT-SE actuaries share indices.

The FT-SE 100 Share Index is the most widely used barometer of stockmarket ups and downs. It reflects the combined performance of the shares of the 100 largest companies quoted on the stockmarket. The table shows the current level, the highs and lows and levels at other specified dates. It also carries the average dividend yield and percentage ratio for the top 100 shares.

There are other indices as well. The FT-SE 250 charts the combined performance of the next 250 largest stockmarket companies below the top 100; while the FT Actuaries All Share Index shows the daily performance of the top-800 companies. It is a broader measure of stockmarket movements. And it forms the basis for the whole series of indices which reflect the price movements of shares in different sectors.

Sector indices.

Indices like the FT-SE 100 show you what the stockmarket is doing overall. But within that, shares in the various industrial groups may follow a different pattern. That is reflected in the various sector indices, which show the average movement of shares in that group plus the group's average dividend yield and price/earnings ratio.

All these different indices help investors to decide whether an individual share is worth buying, if it's time to sell and how well their portfolio is doing against the stockmarket as a whole.

Relative performance.

As you begin to follow the stockmarket more closely you will find that the professionals talk a lot about the "relative performance" of shares as well as the overall trend. You will hear phrases such as "this share is undervalued" or "that share is overvalued". Different sectors and companies may be "due for a re-rating". The shrewd investor wants to buy shares that are likely to outperform the rest of the stockmarket – that is, do better relative to the rest. The various indices we have outlined above act as benchmarks by which to assess individual share performance – and can help pin-point shares that may outperform the rest.

Say you spot a share in the food retailing sector. You have looked at the accounts and decided that it is a good or growing business. But before you buy you want to find out a bit more about the likely performance of the shares.

Price/earnings ratio.

Is the price/earnings (p/e) ratio high or low compared with the sector average? It's low. That is interesting – but it does not mean that the shares are undervalued. A lower than average p/e ratio can indicate a number of things.

It might mean profits are expected to be down this year – when you work out the p/e ratio on the basis of reduced earnings per share you may find it's bang on the average.

Or it could mean that even if profits are growing they may be doing so at a slower rate then other food retailers.

The company may be small and therefore considered more vulnerable – compare the market capitalisation with the higher rated companies in the sector – bigger companies may command a higher p/e ratio.

That is not to say the shares are not worth buying – it merely demonstrates that the p/e ratio reflects what the stockmarket feels about the shares. It is not expecting particularly scintillating profits growth. But feelings can change – so can companies.

If the company is entering a period of above average profits growth then there may indeed be a "re-rating" of the shares in the future – this is the sort of thing every investor hopes to stumble on.

Maybe the share you fancy has a high p/e ratio relative to the sector. This does not mean it is overvalued – it usually reflects the fact that the company has had consistently higher than average profits and earnings growth – so far. What you have to judge is whether this is going to continue. Shares get re-rated down as well as up – a high p/e ratio makes them very vulnerable if profits fall short of expectations.

The private investor has to bear in mind the massive amount of research that goes on in the City. Stockbrokers' analysts and institutional investors are well placed to keep an eye on what is happening to leading companies. It's unlikely that you will come across a seriously undervalued Blue Chip share for instance that no one else has spotted – these companies are monitored very closely by the analysts.

But the different sectors – and the major companies within them – do respond to shifts in the economic cycle. At the first sign of a recovery you might find that retail shares and house building

shares are among the first to start moving upwards as the stockmarket anticipates a rise in consumer spending. That may be followed by a rise in the share prices of companies which supply the stores and make building materials – and so will benefit from increased demand.

There may be a fashion for certain industries, often new ones, which look as if they are going to grow very fast over the next few years. The sector indices are a useful tool that show you what the stockmarket feels about that particular industrial grouping. Combined with your own judgement about future economic trends it helps you decide if it is likely to underperform or outperform the stockmarket.

In Chapter Three we suggested that you pick a few shares for a hypothetical portfolio – monitoring them to see how they perform. Now is a good time to assess progress. You can compare your portfolio as a whole with the FT-SE 100 Index – would your shares have done better, worse, or kept up with the stockmarket average over the last few months?

Then have a look at each individual share. Did it respond to general news on the economy in the way you expected; or to any results it may have announced meanwhile?

Now you have much more knowledge about the way the stockmarket works and values shares. Apply that to your hypothetical portfolio. Why have some shares done better than others? Are your original assumptions proving correct? Think about it carefully.

8

Beginner's guide to gilts.

Shares are not the only kind of investment traded on the stockmarket. Government securities – or gilts as they are known – account for a large slice of daily market activity. But what are gilts? How do they differ from shares? What part can they play in your investment portfolio?

Gilts are a form of government borrowing. Selling gilts is one of the ways the government raises money to fund its spending programme. They may also be called government bonds.

Gilts are always traded in units of £100 nominal (or face value). They offer investors a fixed interest return – in the form of twice yearly payments – and the promise of repayment of the nominal capital at a specified date. But it is important to understand that while government backing makes them secure investments with a certain and quantifiable return, gilts are not risk free. Once they have been issued, prices go up and down on the stockmarket. The key factors which make gilt prices move are the level of interest rates and the rate of inflation. Timing and anticipation are important when investing in gilts. In broad outline, prices rise when interest rates fall, and fall when interest rates rise.

Investors can use gilts in two main ways:

- To secure a fixed return on their money over a number of years.
- To make a capital gain by buying gilts when prices are low and selling when they rise.

Before we look at how gilts may fit into your own investment plans it is important to understand the mechanics – and the jargon – of the gilts market.

Specimen Gilts Page from the *Financial Times*

Interest Yield

Redemption Yield

UK GILTS PRICES

Notes	Yield Int	Yield Red	Price £	+ or –	1993/94 High	1993/94 Low
Shorts" (Lives up to Five Years)						
Treas 14 1/2pc 1994‡‡	14.50	–	100xd	....	109 1/4	100
Exch 13 1/2pc 1994	13.28	5.00	101 21/32	....	109 5/16	101 21/32
Treas. 10pc Ln. 1994‡‡	9.85	5.03	101 9/16	....	105 21/32	101 9/16
Exch 12 1/2pc 1994	12.03	4.98	103 7/8xd	....	110 3/32	103 7/8
Treas 9pc 1994‡‡	8.74	4.95	102 15/16	....	105 21/32	102 15/16
12pc 1995	11.27	4.93	106 13/32	....	111 15/32	106 13/32
Exch 3pc Gas 90–95	3.06	4.79	98	....	98	94
10 1/4pc 1995 *(Example (B))*	9.57	5.09	107 3/32	....	109 7/8	107
Treas 12 3/4pc 1995‡‡	11.33	5.19	112 1/2	....	116 7/8	112 13/32
14pc 1996	12.09	5.31	115 13/16	....	120 5/8	115 3/4
15 1/4pc 1996‡‡	12.68	5.41	120 5/16	....	125 5/8	120 5/16
Exch 13 1/4pc 1996‡‡	11.39	5.44	116 11/32	–1/32	120 1/16	115 1/4
Conversion 10pc 1996	9.01	5.63	111	....	112 5/8	108 7/8
Treas 13 1/4pc 1997‡‡	11.05	5.78	119 29/32	–1/32	122 9/16	118 1/2
Exch 10 1/2pc 1997	9.30	5.77	112 15/16xd	–1/16	114 21/32	110 9/16
Treas 8 3/4pc 1997‡‡	8.01	5.85	109 1/4xd	....	110 7/8	105 1/2
Exch 15pc 1997	11.59	6.00	129 7/16	–1/8	132 11/32	127 15/16
9 3/4pc 1998 *(Example (A))*	8.63	6.01	112 13/16	–1/8	114 13/16	109 1/16
Treas 7 1/4pc 1998‡‡	6.92	5.96	104 23/32	–5/32	106 9/32	99 21/32
7 1/4pc 1998 B‡‡	6.93	5.97	104 21/32	–5/32	106 7/32	101 23/32
Treas 6 3/4pc 1995–98‡‡	6.64	5.30	101 23/32	....	102 1/4	97 21/32
14pc '98–1	10.86	6.18	128 15/16	–1/8	131 5/8	125 1/16
Treas 15 1/2pc '98‡‡	11.28	6.09	137 3/8	–9/32	140 11/32	133 23/32
Exch 12pc 1998	9.72	6.23	123 7/16	–1/16	126 3/16	118 3/8
Treas 9 1/2pc 1999‡‡	8.33	6.15	114	–1/8	116 3/16	108 5/16
Five to Fifteen Years						
Exch 12 1/4pc 1999	9.76	6.32	125 9/16	–1/16	128 1/2	120 3/16
Treas 10 1/2pc 1999	8.84	6.26	118 3/4	–1/8	121 3/8	112 31/32
Treas 6pc 1999 ‡‡	6.01	6.03	99 27/32	–1/8	101 21/32	98 1/4
Conversion 10 1/4pc 1999	8.64	6.34	118 19/32	–3/32	121 1/2	112 7/16
9pc 2000‡‡	7.94	6.30	113 11/32xd	–1/16	116 1/4	106
Treas 13pc 2000	9.75	6.55	133 5/16	....	136 13/16	125 1/2
10pc 2001	8.42	6.62	118 13/16xd	–1/32	122 5/32	109 15/16
7pc '01 ‡‡	6.78	6.48	103 3/16	–1/32	106 5/16	97 27/32
9 3/4pc 2002	8.17	6.73	119 3/8xd	–3/32	123 5/16	108 3/8
8pc 2003‡‡	7.29	6.58	109 23/32	....	113 21/32	97 9/16
10pc 2003	8.15	6.73	122 21/32xd	–1/32	127 3/16	109 5/8
Treas 11 1/2pc 2001–4	9.12	6.80	126 3/32xd	–1/16	129 19/32	116 7/8
Funding 3 1/2pc '99–4	4.26	5.81	82 1/8	–1/16	86 5/32	67 15/16
Conversion 9 1/2pc 2004	7.90	6.79	120 5/16	–1/8	125 13/32	105 7/8
Treas 6 3/4pc 2004‡‡	6.66	6.57	101 9/32	–1/16	105 5/32	97 3/4
6 3/4pc 2004 A	6.67	6.59	101 5/32	....	104 7/8	100 1/4
Conv 9 1/2 pc 2005	7.87	6.81	120 25/32	–1/16	125 11/16	105 7/8
Treas 12 1/2pc 2003–5	9.01	6.96	138 11/16	–3/32	143 23/32	124 3/16
7 3/4pc 2006‡‡	7.18	6.79	107 15/16xd	–1/8	112 19/32	94 17/32
8pc 2002–6‡‡	7.45	6.80	107 7/16	–1/16	111 7/8	94 7/16
Treas 11 3/4pc 2003–7	8.94	6.95	131 1/2	–1/8	136 5/16	118 17/32
Treas 8 1/2pc 2007 ‡‡	7.43	6.84	114 7/16	–3/32	119 11/32	97 5/16
13 1/2pc '04–8	9.19	6.96	146 27/32	–1/8	151 23/32	131 5/16
Treas 9pc 2008 ‡‡	7.52	6.85	119 21/32	–3/32	124 23/32	101 1/4
Over Fifteen Years						
Treas 8pc 2009	7.24	6.86	110 9/16	+1/32	115 25/32	92 3/16
Treas 6 1/4pc 2010 (£50p/paid)	7.13	6.78	44 21/32	–1/32	48 3/32	44 1/16
Conv 9pc Ln 2011 ‡‡	7.41	6.86	121 15/32	–3/32	126 25/32	100 1/2
Treas 9pc 2012‡‡	7.36	6.86	122 1/4	–1/16	127 11/16	100 7/16
Treas 5 1/2pc 2008–12‡‡	6.23	6.61	88 5/16xd	....	94	70 1/4
Treas 8pc 2013‡‡	7.12	6.84	112 5/16	–1/16	117 3/4	93 27/32
7 3/4pc 2012–15‡‡	7.10	6.81	109 1/8	–7/8	114 3/4	89 5/8
Treas 8 3/4pc 2017‡‡	7.14	6.81	122 17/32xd	–1/16	128 3/4	97 1/16
Exch 12pc '13–'17	7.86	7.02	152 3/4	–1/16	159 1/2	125 29/32
Undated						
Consols 4pc	7.06	–	56 5/8	+1/4	60	43 5/8
War Loan 3 1/2pc‡‡	6.87	–	50 15/16	–3/32	54 13/32	38 5/8
Conv 3 1/2pc '61 Aft.	5.22	–	67 1/16	–9/16	71	60 7/8
Treas 3pc '66 Aft.	7.25	–	41 3/8	–1/4	44 5/8	33 1/2
Consols 2 1/2pc	7.07	–	35 3/8	–1/4	38 1/2	28 5/8
Treas. 2 1/2pc	7.07	–	35 3/8	+1/4	37 5/8	27 13/16

Notes	Yield (1)	Yield (2)	Price £	+ or –	1993/94 High	1993/94 Low
Index–Linked (b)						
Treas. 2pc '94 (102.9)	–	–	137 1/8	....	137 1/8	131 5/8
2pc '96 (67.9)	1.36	2.28	202 7/16xd	–5/16	204 1/2	194 11/16
4 5/8pc '98‡‡ (135.6)	1.64	2.28	111 1/2	–3/16	113 9/16	105 9/16
2 1/2pc '01 (78.3)	2.32	2.67	174 9/16xd	–3/8	176 7/8	159
2 1/2pc '03 (78.8)	2.54	2.82	171 1/8	–3/8	173 5/8	155
4 3/8pc '04‡‡ (135.6)	2.58	2.86	116 3/16	–5/16	118 1/2	105 1/2
2pc '06 (69.5)	2.67	2.89	180 13/16	–9/16	184 9/16	159 1/4
2 1/2pc '09 (78.8)	2.86	3.05	163 7/8	–9/16	168 7/16	144
2 1/2pc '11 (74.6)	2.91	3.08	170 15/16xd	–9/16	175 11/16	148 13/16
2 1/2pc '13 (89.2)	2.95	3.10	141 9/16	–9/16	146 1/4	122 5/16
2 1/2pc '16 (81.6)	3.00	3.14	151 7/8	–5/8	157 1/4	130 15/32
2 1/2pc '20 (83.0)	3.05	3.17	146 15/16	–5/8	152 11/16	124 23/32
2 1/2pc '24‡‡ (97.7)	3.03	3.15	123 7/8	–9/16	129 1/8	102 5/8
4 1/8pc '30‡‡ (135.1)	3.05	3.17	123 1/2	–9/16	128 13/16	103 3/4

Prospective real redemption rate on projected inflation of (1) 10% and (2) 5%. (b) Figures in parentheses show RPI base for indexing (ie 8 months prior to issue) and have been adjusted to reflect rebasing of RPI to 100 in January 1987. Conversion factor 3.945. RPI for May 1993: 141.1 and for December 1993: 141.9.

Other Fixed Interest

Notes	Yield Int	Yield Red	Price £	+ or –	1993/94 High	1993/94 Low
African Dev 11 1/8 2010	8.11	7.17	137 1/8	....	142 9/16	115 7/8
Asian Dev 10 1/4pc 2009	8.00	7.17	128 1/8	+1/32	138 3/8	108 31/32
B'ham 11 1/2pc 2012	8.41	7.76	136 3/4	–1/4	142	114
Ireland Cap 8 1/2pc '10	7.56	–	112 1/2	....	120	95
9pc Cap 1996	8.76	–	102 3/4	....	116	97 1/2
13pc '97–2	11.40	–	114	....	130	110
Hydro Quebec 15pc 2011	9.16	8.07	163 27/32	....	170 1/32	139 5/16
Leeds 13 1/2pc 2006	9.29	–	145 1/4	....	149 3/4	128
Liverpool 3 1/2pc Irred.	8.09	–	43 1/4	....	44 3/4	34
LCC 3pc '20 Aft.	7.69	–	39	+1/4	40 1/2	30 1/2
Manchester 11 1/2pc 2007	8.75	7.73	131 1/2	....	136 1/4	114
Met. Wtr. 3pc 'B'	3.97	6.59	75 1/2	....	78	63 1/4
N'wide Anglia 3 7/8pc 2021	–	3.84	146	....	150 3/4	117 1/2
4 1/4pc IL 2024	–	3.82	140 3/4	+1/4	145 1/4	115 1/2
Utd Mex States 16 1/2pc 2008	10.68	–	154 1/2	–1/4	159 1/2	132 1/4

● 'Tap' stock. ‡‡ Tax-free to non-residents on application. E Auction basis. xd Ex dividend. Closing mid-prices are shown in pounds.

Gilt prices are shown in the daily financial section of most newspapers. In the *Financial Times* they are listed as British funds. The daily listings provide you with crucial information. As you will see from our illustration on page 69, each gilt has a coupon – the rate of interest paid on each £100 nominal stock issued, and a redemption date – when that £100 will be paid back.

Confusingly, the coupon is not the real guide to the actual return investors get from a gilt – that depends on the price you pay for it. The price you will see in the daily lists is what you pay for £100 nominal of gilt stock on the stockmarket. So to find out what your return would be at the current price, you must look further along the columns where you will see two kinds of yields.

The interest yield tells you what return you get buying the gilt at the current market price. This is also known as the flat yield.

The redemption yield tells you what you get when buying the gilt at the current market price and holding until it is repaid. The redemption yield takes into account the capital gains or losses made by investors on repayment, as well as the interest paid. It shows you the total return.

Two examples.

Looking at our illustration on page 69, you will see that Exchequer 15% 1997 (Example A) is priced at £129$^{7}/_{16}$ on the stockmarket. All gilt prices are in pounds, not pence. The coupon is 15% – that is the amount of interest you will receive on each £100 nominal of stock. But you are paying more than that nominal amount, so your actual return will be less – it will in fact work out at 11.59%. That is the interest yield or flat yield.

The stock for which you have paid £129$^{7}/_{16}$ will be repaid at its nominal value of £100 in 1997 – so you will have a capital loss of £29$^{7}/_{16}$ if you hold it until then. If you take that into account, your rate of return is reduced to 6% if you hold until repayment. That is the redemption yield.

Exchequer 15% 1997 is a high-coupon gilt – the return is in the form of annual interest. As you look over the list we reproduce on page 69, you may wonder why anyone would want to buy a low-coupon gilt – like Exchequer 3% Gas 90-95 (Example B) for instance. But in the case of low-coupon gilts, the investment attraction is that what you may lose in interest, you make up as an assured return in the form of capital gain. This gilt is priced at £98 – below nominal value. It will be repaid at £100 in 1995 at the latest. So while the interest yield is 3.06%, the redemption yield is higher at 4.79%, reflecting this capital gain. Since capital gains on gilts are tax exempt, low-coupon gilts are particularly attractive to higher-rate taxpayers.

Interest rates are actually calculated day by day. But the information provided by the daily financial press does the important sums for you. You have to understand what the figures mean – and also the characteristics of the main categories of gilts you will see listed.

- Short-dated gilts are those with less than five years to redemption.
- Medium-dated gilts are those with redemption dates of between five and 15 years.
- Long-dated gilts are those with over 15 years to redemption.
- Undated gilts have no set repayment date, and in practice are unlikely ever to be repaid. Take specialist advice before thinking of buying them.
- Index-linked gilts are relatively new. The interest paid and repayment are linked to the Retail Price Index.

The length of time to repayment is an important factor in gilt prices. "Shorts" for instance are more sensitive to the current level of interest rates.

Investors may compare the return on the short-dated gilt with what they might get from a building society or some other income generating investment that matures within a few years.

"Longs" and "mediums" are more difficult to judge since they require a degree of crystal ball gazing. While they offer the investor an assured fixed income for a number of years, you have to think carefully about the future level of both interest rates and inflation – particularly if you intend holding until redemption.

Usually you will find that the longer-dated gilts offer highest yields – reflecting the normal investment rule that the longer you "tie up" your money, the higher the return. But you can get an "inverse" yield curve where "shorts" are showing higher yields. This indicates that interest rates are expected to fall – the lower yields on "longs" reflect what the stockmarket thinks will happen in the future.

High inflation is not good news for conventional gilts, nor any fixed-income investment, because it eats into the real value of the income – and the real value of the capital at redemption.

High inflation inevitably means that gilt prices fall since yields must rise to compensate for the reduction in real returns.

Timing is also important when it comes to interest rates. If you go into gilts when interest rates are low, you stand to lose out when they rise because your return is "fixed" when you buy – so you are missing out on a better deal – and the market price for gilts will go down as interest rates rise. When you consider the ups and downs in interest rates over the past few years you will see why gilts can be a very volatile investment despite their "safe" image.

The best time to buy gilts is when interest rates are high – and expected to fall. That way you secure a high fixed return (either in the form of income or capital) and have the option of taking a capital gain by selling your stock when interest rates fall and the market price rises.

Most investors who buy gilts are less interested in "playing the market" by buying and selling gilts than in having a proportion of their portfolio with a guaranteed return on a medium to long term basis.

Choosing gilts.

Which gilts you buy depends on your investment objectives – and your tax situation.

Investors wanting high income should look for a high coupon gilt with a good interest yield and a redemption date that reflects the length of time you plan to invest for. If you retire at 60, for instance, and need a good income from your investments over the next 15 to 20 years you will find an appropriately dated gilt among the "longs" listed. There will be a capital loss if you hold to redemption – but that may be acceptable if your priority is maximising the ongoing income from your investments. There may be less point in the high-income seeker buying short-dated gilts – even if the yield happens to be higher. But there can be no absolute rule. This is a complex subject, crucially influenced by timing, and you usually need to take expert advice.

For investors paying higher rate tax who do not need an immediate high income, low-coupon gilts are more attractive since most of the return will be in the form of a capital gain when the nominal amount is paid back rather than the annual interest. Capital gains on gilts are tax exempt and low coupon gilts can be a useful part of a growth portfolio.

While undated gilts are best left to the experts, carefully chosen index-linked gilts guarantee investors a "real" return over and above the rate of inflation. Both the capital repayment and interest payments are linked to the movement of the

Retail Price Index, so they offer the certainty of beating inflation. Once again, this is a complicated subject which needs specialist advice.

Buying gilts.

You can buy gilts through a stockbroker, financial adviser or a bank. As in the case of shares there will be a minimum charge which will vary according to where you buy them. But by far the cheapest way for the private investor to buy gilts is at the Post Office – though you won't get advice on which gilt to buy.

Most Post Offices carry a list of gilts on the National Savings Stock Register – ask for details (there are leaflets available) at the counter. Most gilts are on it. By this method, you will pay £1 commission if you are buying under £250 worth and then another £1 for each £250 worth you purchase.

Another advantage is that the interest on gilts bought through the Post Office is paid gross, that is, without deduction of tax.

Non taxpayers should buy their gilts this way – though if you are a taxpayer you will have to declare the interest and pay tax on it eventually. If you buy your gilts through the stockmarket, tax is deducted from your interest cheque before you receive it.

What is a unit trust?

A unit trust is a fund that invests in shares. When you buy "units" you are acquiring not the underlying shares but a stake in the whole fund which may own dozens of holdings in different companies quoted on the stockmarket. A unit trust's investments are looked after by professional managers who decide which shares to buy and sell. Unit trusts are often described as "open ended". As investors buy units, the size of the fund increases as it has more money to invest. If they sell units, the underlying investments can be sold. In practice in normal markets there is a two-way traffic in units. Your stockbroker or financial adviser will be happy to make recommendations and buy the units for you.

Unit trusts versus shares.

Over the last 30 years unit trusts have been very popular with investors – even at times when fewer private individuals were buying individual shares. One of their main advantages is that they offer the small investors a good spread of investments at a reasonable cost.

Say you have £1,000 to put into the stockmarket. Because you have to pay a minimum commission each time it will be expensive for you to buy more than a couple of different shares. Maybe you are nervous about putting all the money in one or two companies. You might buy a unit trust instead – that will give you a stake in the wider range of stockmarket companies and you won't have to pay several lots of commission.

Unit trusts have another important advantage – they offer you an easy way of investing abroad. Buying individual shares in overseas companies is a bit daunting – but there are strong arguments for having some part of your investments in overseas stockmarkets. You would find it difficult to get into the Far Eastern stockmarkets, for instance, in any other way.

The major disadvantage is that putting all your portfolio into unit trusts takes a lot of the fun out of choosing your own stockmarket investments. And because funds invest in many different companies, no unit trust is likely to equal the performance of one real stockmarket winner – or indeed a real stockmarket disaster.

Picking unit trusts.

Because there are so many funds this is almost as tricky as picking shares. The monthly magazine *Money Management* carries the most comprehensive list of what is available and publishes a formidable array of performance statistics. You will see that the funds are divided into a number of different sectors – there is a wide range and they offer very different kinds of investment possibilities.

Even if you just want to buy into the British stockmarket there is a baffling number – growth funds, income funds,

smaller company funds. There are international funds with shares in most of the overseas stockmarkets – and unit trusts that invest in just one region – North America for instance, or Japan. There are the highly specialised funds investing in gold shares, or property – or recovery funds where the managers select shares that have had a bad time but which they believe will now do well. And if you are really confused, there are unit trusts that invest in other unit trusts within the same investment management group – these are known as funds of funds. How on earth do you start? As with buying shares you have to decide what kind of investment or combination of investments you are looking for.

If you want long-term capital growth look first at the UK general and UK growth unit trusts. These make a sensible basis for any unit trust portfolio. Pick a broadly based fund that has performed well and steadily over the last few years.

These funds will rarely feature among the top industry performers. But if you want a solid investment this is where you should start.

If income is important there are plenty of UK equity income unit trusts that invest in shares with above average yields – and give you capital growth as well.

International unit trusts are the best way to get a stake in a wide range of overseas stockmarkets. It means that your portfolio is not entirely dependent on what happens at home. But you should be aware that exchange rates can have a big impact on the value of your investments too. This is particularly important if you invest in just one country or region.

These unit trusts should be considered long-term investments, making up the core of your portfolio. More active investors who are prepared to take a greater risk with part of their money should look at the specialist unit trusts on offer.

You will find recovery funds in the UK growth sector. Managers of these will be looking for "bombed out" shares with recovery potential – particularly interesting as the economy climbs out of recession.

UK smaller companies are another, more volatile sector – these often do well in the final stages of a stockmarket boom.

Other cyclical sectors that you can invest in through unit trusts include property and gold shares.

One country or region funds are another possibility. Remember that the narrower the investment range the more volatile the fund can be.

With these specialist funds, timing is all important. If you manage to buy at the bottom and sell at the top you can make handsome profits. Get it wrong and you can make hefty losses.

You must know about the sector, be prepared to take a bit of a gamble – and be ready to sell if you think it the right thing to do. Above all don't commit more than a small proportion of your portfolio, a quarter say, to this kind of fund.

Costs.

The cost of investing in a unit trust is included in the initial price you pay for your "units". The difference between the

offer price at which you buy and the bid price at which you sell is usually 6% – 7%. This spread covers the manager's own dealing expenses, and commission. In addition there is an annual charge – between 1% and 1½%. It is a mistake to assume that it is always cheaper to buy unit trusts rather than shares – much depends on the size and spread of your personal portfolio.

Investment trusts.

Like unit trusts, investment trusts offer investors a way of spreading their stockmarket risks through pooled or collective investment. Like unit trusts, investment trusts manage a portfolio of shares. Like unit trusts, investment trusts offer a convenient route to overseas stockmarkets.

Like unit trusts, investment trusts offer a good range of investment possibilities – from reliable general funds covering the whole of the stockmarket to more specialist categories of investment. But there are important differences.

Investment trusts have shares that are quoted on the stockmarket. What determines the price of those shares is not the value of their underlying portfolio as in the case of unit trusts, but the demand for them on the stockmarket. This complication explains why they have not, until recently, been so popular with small investors. The price of a unit trust "unit" directly reflects the stockmarket value of its portfolio. An investment trust share, on the other hand, usually sells at a discount to the value of its portfolio. The size of this discount can vary. That introduces an element of uncertainty into the investment equation. When investment trust shares were out of fashion a few years ago, the discounts grew very large – a third or more. Nowadays they are much smaller, reflecting their increasing popularity with investors.

Naturally the shares of well managed trusts where the fund managers have increased the value of their portfolio by skilful investment are in demand – the shares will go up as the value of the portfolio rises. In addition, the discount will narrow, so there is a double gain. Obviously the discount means there is an element of extra risk, too – discounts can widen as well as shrink. Investment trust shares do broadly follow the progress of their underlying share portfolios. And they have some advantages over unit trusts.

Investment trusts can borrow money to invest. This gives investors greater growth potential – and higher risks. They can also invest in unquoted companies although these can be riskier investments. Investment trusts can be attractive take-over targets when their assets are worth substantially more than the market value of their shares.

Investment trusts have lower management charges. The bid/offer spread for a large trust may be less than 3%. Shares are bought through the stockmarket – on larger bargains costs should be lower than buying a comparable unit trust.

Your stockbroker will certainly be able to give you advice on what to buy. *Money Management* magazine compiles monthly performance tables and divides the trusts into sectors. As with unit trusts, your choice boils down to defining your investment profile and what kind of funds, or mixture of funds, are suitable for you. The same general rules apply.

The Association of Unit Trusts and Investment Funds (071-831 0898) and the Association of Investment Trust Companies (071-588 5347) have helpful leaflets for potential investors.

10

Tax-free investments.

Over the past few years the government has been keen to stimulate personal savings and investment. The result is the introduction of tax concessions for certain kinds of investments. The principle behind this is that savers who invest up to a maximum sum for a minimum period pay no tax on the proceeds – encouraging them to build up a nest egg on a long-term basis.

Personal equity plans (PEPs) enable you to invest in the stockmarket and pay no income tax on your share dividends or Capital Gains Tax on your profits. While no one should invest simply because of a tax concession, it may make sense to make some or all of your share investments through a PEP.

PEPs are offered by stockbrokers, financial advisers, unit and investment trusts and financial services companies.

How much can you invest?

The PEP rules have changed somewhat since 1987 when the tax concessions were first introduced – and may change from Budget to Budget. At the moment, each individual investor can put up to £6,000 a year in a general PEP – investing in a number of different shares or unit and investment trusts. And you can put a further £3,000 a year in what is known as a single company or corporate PEP – many Stock Exchange companies now have their own schemes. If you don't use your maximum PEP "allocation" each tax year you can't invest more than your allowance in the next.

Investments must be in UK shares or an EC stockmarket – unit and investment trusts must have at least 50% of their portfolios invested in these to be included in a PEP. You can't put existing holdings into a PEP – it has to be a new investment.

Provided you hold the PEP for a year, dividends and capital profits are tax free.

Who should invest in a PEP?

Investors should look very hard at the level of charges before deciding to invest through a PEP – as these could swallow a lot of the "tax-free" advantages. On the other hand, anyone who is investing substantial amounts

each year in a PEP stands to gain a lot from the tax concessions over the longer term.

- Everyone is entitled to £5,800 of capital gains a year before they are liable to pay any Capital Gains Tax (CGT). So the PEP tax concession is only relevant if you think you may realise profits of more than that on your shares. It sounds a lot now. But if you are investing substantial amounts in the stockmarket each year you could be building up a big tax liability for the future. That is when the PEP comes into its own.
- High-rate taxpayers obviously benefit the most from the tax concession on income from PEP investments. It's worth remembering that, provided the investments remain in the PEP, the income is tax free forever. That makes a PEP an important part of any long-term retirement planning. A PEP is a good alternative, for instance, to making additional voluntary contributions into a pension plan. You will pay income tax on pension payments – but none on the return from your PEP, which has the extra advantage of giving you access to your cash.

Choosing a PEP.

If you want a good spread of investments a general PEP is your best choice and there is a wide variety.

- Are you looking for income? Some PEPs pay income quarterly or monthly.
- Are you looking for growth? – like unit and investment trusts, different plans have different investment objectives.
- Do you want just individual shares in your PEP?

- Do you want to put the lot into unit or investment trusts – or a mixture of these and shares?
- Do you want a "managed" PEP where investments are chosen for you by the managers?
- Do you want a "self select" PEP which gives you a choice of shares?
- Do you want to make monthly contributions into a PEP instead of a lump sum investment? Some managers offer this facility.

With a "managed" PEP, you should look for one with a good track record. Investment performance is more important than the level of charges in the long term.

With a "self select" PEP, you want one that allows you to switch investments cheaply and easily. These are offered by many stockbrokers.

You should also look for a PEP that complements your existing investments. If you already have unit trusts, for instance, you might use your PEP to invest in individual shares (maybe on a self select basis). If you have just a few shares you might get a better spread by holding unit or investment trusts in your PEP.

Single-company PEP.

In addition to the £6,000 a year you can put into a general PEP, you can invest £3,000 a year in a single-company or corporate PEP. Originally these were designed to enable employee shareholders to put existing shares into a PEP. But any investor can take one out. The charges are low compared with managed PEPs – and you can switch companies within a year without losing the tax advantages.

Other investments that offer tax concessions.

A TESSA (tax-exempt special savings account) is a bank or building society deposit account. You can save up to £9,000 tax free in a TESSA provided you keep the cash there for five years. You can invest up to £3,000 in the first year and up to £1,800 in the three following years and £600 in the final year. You will pay no tax on the interest. You can't withdraw capital without sacrificing the tax concessions, but you can get the interest, net of tax – the tax is repaid after five years.

- Look for the highest rate available. But remember that the rate goes up or down – there are very few fixed-rate schemes.
- Watch out for high "penalty" charges on some accounts if you switch your TESSA to get a better rate.
- You don't have to make a lump sum investment. Many banks and building societies offer monthly savings into a TESSA.

National Savings has a variety of products, some of which offer tax-free investments. The advantage of National Savings Certificates is that they offer a guaranteed return over five years. Check to see if rates are competitive with what is on offer elsewhere – because there is no commission, financial advisers may not bother to recommend what can often be a very attractive deal for higher-rate taxpayers. National Savings products are available over the counter at Post Offices.

11

Personal pensions.

It cannot be said too often. A pension is one of the most important aspects of financial planning. Like your mortgage, your insurances and your "rainy day" cash, making sure that you will have enough money in retirement must be a top priority – it is a cornerstone of your overall savings strategy. Even if you are already contributing to an employer's pension scheme – and happy to stay there – you should look carefully to see if you should make extra pension provision. If you're not, you should think seriously about investing in a personal pension plan.

The government has been keen to promote the savings habit. When it comes to personal pensions the tax incentives are very generous indeed giving us plenty of incentive to save now for later. Not surprisingly this has spawned a huge pensions industry – there are plenty of salesmen around enticing you to buy this or that plan. It can all be very confusing – independent advice is often hard to come by. But here are a few general pension points to ponder.

Start early if you want to make sure of building up a decent pension to retire on. Each year you delay means that it will cost you more to create the same amount of pension at the end of the day. The sooner you invest the money the more opportunity you have for your pension savings to grow over the years.

Inflation may be low now but it is still a vital factor in assessing the real value of your future pension. Basic living costs will rise by the time you come to retire. What will that do to the spending power of what you are expecting to receive when you stop earning?

Your dependants will need to be looked after financially whether you die before or after retirement. Whatever pension scheme you choose you must look carefully at these arrangements as well.

Personal pensions.

Everyone is now entitled to have a personal pension plan – even if they work for an employer that offers a pension scheme. One of the most difficult decisions is whether to join a company scheme, or to opt for the personal pension plans sold by a large number of insurance companies, investment houses, banks and other financial institutions. It is important to understand the basic differences between the two.

Company pensions will typically offer a pension based on your salary when you retire. Both you and the employer will contribute a percentage of your earnings to the fund. There will be a range of other benefits too – a widow's or widower's pension for instance and a life insurance payment to dependants if you die before retirement, plus, maybe, increases in the value of your pension once it is being paid. These are the plus points.

The main disadvantage is when you change jobs – the structure of company pension schemes favours those who remain in the same employment for a long time. Even though you can now take the "transfer value" of your pension to a new employer you may still lose out. Frequent job changes mean that you can end up with bits of pension from a number of past employers. On the other hand a company pension scheme is usually very good value for older employees who don't expect to move jobs. No one should opt out of an employer's scheme without taking independent advice. Most people are better off staying put.

Personal pensions are best for the young who expect to change jobs several times during their working lives. And they are essential if there is no employer's scheme on offer with your job – or if you are self-employed. A personal pension means that you have your own individual "pot" of money that you can contribute to as and how you like regardless of who you are working for – and you can start drawing your pension at the age of 50. The main disadvantage is that the employer does not contribute to the pension (though there is nothing to stop them doing so if you can negotiate it). And there is no guaranteed level of pension. What you get depends on the amount of pension that your "pension pot" can buy you when you retire rather than on the amount of your salary.

Choosing a personal pension.

There is a baffling range of personal pension plans on the market. And since the size of your pension depends on the amount of money you can build up it is important to choose carefully. The first thing to consider is how you want your pension money, or premiums, invested.

Unit-linked pension plans give you a choice of different kinds of funds managed by the insurance or investment company. Typically there will be a wide range of equity funds where money is invested on the stockmarket. These will include overseas shares – there will probably be a Far East or North American fund into which you can put your money.

There will probably be a property fund, a fixed-interest and cash fund – and a managed fund which invests across the whole range – useful if you can't decide which to choose.

Clearly you want to look hard at the investment performance of these funds – bearing in mind that short-term ups and downs may not mean very much when you are tucking away money for the long haul. The further it is until retirement the more risk you may be prepared to take – investing in equity funds for instance. But the nearer you get to retirement the more predictability you need – then is the time to secure your stockmarket gains by putting your money in the cash fund for instance. You can switch your money between different funds. If you go the unit-linked route you will need all your investment knowledge to make the most of your money.

With-profits pensions plans invest the premiums in the insurance or investment company's own fund – which will be a mixture of shares, gilts and maybe property. You will be guaranteed a minimum amount, plus, each year, a share of the profits of the investment fund. The crucial difference between this and a unit-linked pension plan is that these profits, once given, cannot be taken away – and you should get a final bonus added to your fund when you retire. Again it is important to look at the bonus record of the pension provider – though this is no cast iron guarantee of what will happen in the future.

The ideal way to invest your pension money is to use both types of plan – the unit-linked to give you the opportunity for capital appreciation in the stockmarket – and the with-profits to provide a more secure, predictable investment. It is always sensible to spread the risks when you invest and this principle applies equally to your pension plan.

There is nothing to stop you taking out several different plans though you should enquire about the level of charges, which can vary enormously. But bear in mind that in the long run investment performance will be more important. From the personal discipline point of view a regular-premium policy where you make contributions each month or year is a good idea. But you can make a series of one-off payments through single-premium plans instead – or use them to top up your pension payments as and when you can afford it.

How much to invest?

Sellers of pension plans will present you with a whole battery of figures about how much pension your contributions will buy you in 20 or 30 years' time. It is important to understand that these are only estimates, based on assumptions about investment performance. They are not promises or guarantees. You also have to think about the impact of inflation on the rather attractive amounts of pension that are illustrated. The important point to remember is that the sooner you invest the more chance your pension savings have to increase in value. Even if you can make only modest contributions initially you can increase these later on as you earn more money or have fewer financial responsibilities.

Tax.

One of the most attractive features of saving through a pension scheme is the generous tax concessions – you can get full tax relief on your pension contributions up to a maximum proportion of your earnings. And the older you are the higher the proportion of your income you can pay in under present Inland Revenue rules. For instance, you can get full tax relief on up to 17½% of your taxable earnings if you are 35 or younger – but this proportion rises in stages the older you are – at age 51, for instance, your limit will be 30%. So you should check what your limit is with the taxman.

If you are employed you will make contributions to your personal pension plan net of basic-rate tax and claim any higher-rate tax relief from the taxman. If you are self-employed you will make your contributions gross and claim the tax back on your tax return form.

If you don't invest up to the maximum in the tax year – and few of us do – you can make it up later on when you have more money. You can go back six years and utilise any unused tax allowances as well as getting your maximum tax relief for the current year.

Additional voluntary contributions (AVCs).

If you are in an employer's scheme but you want to put more money into your pension you can do so through an AVC. First you have to look at what percentage of your earnings you are already contributing. You can get full tax relief on extra contributions provided the total that you contribute is not more than 15% of your earnings. Many employers offer an AVC scheme of their own – but you are perfectly entitled to buy an independent one from any insurance or investment company of your choice. If you opt for an employer's AVC there should be no charges – but you should enquire carefully about the terms – exactly what are your extra contributions buying you? If you buy a freestanding AVC from an insurance company you will pay commission – it may be worth it if the benefits look better. Compare deals to find out what is appropriate.

The tax concessions on pension contributions – whether you are taking out a personal pension plan or "topping up" with an AVC – make them very attractive ways of saving money. But while you should make sure you are building up a decent pension, it is a mistake to make this your only form of saving. Pensions are inflexible compared with other kinds of investments. Although you can take some of your money in a lump sum the rest has to be paid as pension. What you get in the end depends on how long you, or your dependants, live.

It is not the same as having, for instance, a portfolio of shares or unit trusts that you can cash in when you want to. For this reason many investors prefer to have a personal equity plan, for instance, rather than an AVC. It is important to strike a balance.

12

Tax.

Never invest in something just because of a tax break. That's good advice. But it doesn't mean that you can completely ignore the tax factor when it comes to your investment strategy – far from it. For a start you will probably be liable for tax on your investment returns. So you need to know the basic rules – and how you can, quite legally, reduce your tax bill by ordering investments in the most efficient way. If you have your own business, or a large investment portfolio, you may have access to professional tax advice – but all investors should have a working knowledge of the way taxation

policies affect them. There are important differences in the tax treatment of the various investment products too.

Tax-free investment means just that – you are not liable for tax on your investment returns. Examples include National Savings products that offer a tax-free return. TESSAs – the tax-exempt special savings accounts offered by banks and building societies – and PEPs – the personal equity plans offered by most financial institutions. Provided you stick to the rules, all gains – whether in the form of income or capital – are tax free to the investor.

You can get tax relief on money you put into some investments – a pension plan for instance. Some investments pay income gross to investors – without the deduction of tax. Examples include the National Savings Investment Account (INVAC), gilt-edged securities bought through the National Savings Stock register at the Post Office and income from offshore deposits. But this does not mean that you are not liable for tax on this investment income – you are, unless your total income is so low that you don't pay tax at all.

Most investment income is paid net to investors – after deduction of basic-rate tax. Examples include dividend payments from shares and interest on bank and building society accounts. If you pay just basic-rate income tax it means that you will have no more to pay. But if your total income means

that you are in the higher tax band (currently 40%) then you will owe an additional amount to the taxman. Non-taxpayers (children, non-earning wives) can claim back the tax deducted from the interest on banks and building society accounts and dividends, or ask for the payments to be made gross before deduction of tax.

Capital Gains Tax (CGT) is payable on the increase in the capital value of your investments when you sell them – shares are the obvious example. The rate of CGT you pay depends on your own top rate of income tax – but generous annual exemptions mean that many individual investors should pay little or no CGT.

This is the basic tax framework. But how does it work out in practice? It's very important that you keep up-to-date records of all your investments – the prices at which you buy and sell shares, the income you receive. If you do that it should not be too difficult to work out how much, if anything, you owe the taxman.

Income tax.

Basic-rate taxpayers will have no more to pay on income from shares, unit trusts or bank and building society accounts – you will receive the income net. In the case of income from shares the dividend payment voucher, which you must be careful to keep, will state the amount of tax deducted. Under the present rules this is 20%, the present level of lower-rate tax – even though your basic rate is 25% you will not owe any more. But you will have to pay tax on any interest received gross – where no tax has been deducted.

Higher-rate taxpayers will be liable for more tax on investment income. Say your actual share dividend payment is £80 after the deduction of 20% tax. The gross amount is £100.

If your top tax rate is 40% your tax liability on it will be £40 – 40% of £100. You have already had £20 deducted – so you will have to pay the tax man another £20. Income from bank or building society accounts will also be taxable at 40%. At present basic-rate tax of 25% is deducted before you receive it. So a higher-rate taxpayer will owe another 15%.

Married couples may be able to reduce their total income-tax bills by organising their investments in a tax-efficient way. The current system of independent taxation means that both partners can claim personal tax allowances. If one partner – for instance a wife looking after children – is not earning it would make sense to transfer income-producing investments into her name. Provided that income is not higher than the level of the personal allowance, she can claim back the basic-rate tax deducted from investment returns. If both partners are earning but only one of them is a higher-rate taxpayer the same principle applies – investments should be organised in such a way that income is paid to the basic-rate taxpayer – reducing the size of the overall tax bill.

Capital Gains Tax is payable on investment profits at your highest rate of income tax. But the rules mean that many private investors should, if they are careful, pay no CGT at all. The key point is the annual CGT exemption – currently £5,800.

- You can make profits of up to that amount during the tax year without paying any CGT at all.
- You can offset any capital losses against your gains in the same tax year. For instance if you have sold shares at £8,000 profit but have taken a £3,000 loss on another holding, your overall profits will be £5,000 – well below the level of the CGT exemption.
- You can offset capital losses against gains in future tax years.
- You can only use the CGT exemption for that current tax year - you can't carry it forward to use in future years.

Capital gains are index-linked for tax purposes. That means the paper profit is reduced by the amount of inflation recorded since the purchase. If you are well within your CGT exemption limits, index-linking the gain is rather academic. If you have any problems consult your tax office – there are helpful booklets available on this and other aspects of taxation.

How to make the best use of the ground rules.

It's important to note that married couples each have their own CGT exemption. Investments should be divided to take full advantage of this generous rule.

Your portfolio should be reviewed carefully towards the end of each tax year in order to use the annual CGT exemption. If you have built up large profits in one share you might want to take them or offset them with some of your losses. It doesn't mean that you have to abandon what you still believe to be a good investment. You can sell them to establish a profit in the current tax year that will use your CGT exemption and then repurchase them. Ask your stockbroker about "bed and breakfasting" – the market term for this widely used procedure.

13

New issues.

Who can forget Sid, the elusive character from the British Gas privatisation ads who seems to have passed into folklore as the typical small investor? Which of us failed to shudder at the bumbling Inspector Morose who appeared on our television screens to promote the sale of British Telecom shares? Over the last few years the government's privatisation policy has succeeded in persuading many of us to become shareholders for the first time, spreading the message that everyone can buy shares – and profit from so doing. British Telecom, British Gas, the regional electricity companies, the water companies – all these are examples of the shares of State enterprises being offered for sale on the stockmarket.

These privatisations are new issues – only much bigger and more widely promoted than most new issues. The new issue is an important feature of the stockmarket – where a company goes public by offering its shares for sale, enabling the owners to capitalise on the firm's success or raise money for the business. Going right back to the basis of the stockmarket, selling equity in your enterprise is the alternative to borrowing money from the bank. The new issue encapsulates the original capital-raising function of the stockmarket – and it has a special appeal to the small investor.

An offer for sale is the most straightforward kind of new issue. Shares are offered to the public at a fixed price. Advertisements are placed in newspapers inviting investors to apply for a prospectus, which gives details of the company. You have a certain amount of time to apply for the shares and send your cheque – and there is a date on which dealing in the shares starts on the stockmarket.

Commission-free shares.

When you apply for shares through an offer for sale you pay no commission – so it's cheaper to acquire them this way than by buying later in the second-hand market. And while an instant profit is not guaranteed you may be sure that the company that is offering the shares, along with its advisers, will be very keen for the new issue to show a profit – known as a premium – when trading in the shares actually starts on the stockmarket. A successful new issue is one where all the shares are taken up and which opens at a profit of between 10% and 20% on the first day of dealing. Any City institution that backs a new issue which fails to give everyone an opening profit has made a mistake by pricing the shares too high.

Of course things go wrong sometimes. Advisers make mistakes – sudden bad economic news can depress the stockmarket in the vital days between announcement and dealings. Sometimes there are not enough investors who fancy the shares – leaving them with the underwriters who agree in advance to take any of the new issue that is left over. When that happens the shares might fall below the issue price when dealings start – which is a serious blow to a company's image and it can depress the share price for a long time. But all this does underline the commitment of companies and their advisers to making sure that the offer is a success, giving the investor who buys a new issue a nice little profit to start off with. Everyone likes to buy at a discount – and that is what you can do if you get shares in a successful new issue.

Privatisations.

Privatisations have followed this pattern. Because they are much larger than other new issues they have been given the full publicity treatment. Often they come with deliberate discounts built in. Some allow shareholders a discount on their bills if they are customers. Or they allow shareholders to pay for the shares by instalments, with a discount on the instalment price and dividends paid in such a way as to ensure that there is a high return on the cash investors have to fork out in the early stages. All of this means that practically every new issue in the privatisation programme has been worth buying, and generally worth holding. Because the companies are new the finances can be structured to ensure a flow of growing profits and dividends in the early years.

The problem with privatisation issues is that they are usually too successful. Almost always they attract such a flood of cash that they are oversubscribed – investors want more shares than are available. Multiple applications are outlawed – no one is allowed to make more than one application for him or herself. But it is perfectly legal for parents to apply on behalf of their children. That establishes quite clearly the first law of successful new issue investment – make as many applications as the law allows. Apply for shares in the name of every member of the family. That way, if for instance there are six of you – mum, dad and four kids – you have six chances of getting shares instead of just one!

In some new issues where there are too many applications, the issuing house simply holds a ballot – a lucky dip – to decide who gets shares and everyone else is excluded. Again, the more separate applications you make the higher your chances. Privatisations, however, are handled differently. Because the government wants to encourage as many investors as possible the shares are spread as widely as possible.

What happens is that the amounts may be drastically scaled down. So it's better to get four small allotments of shares than apply for one big one – that way you will almost certainly get more.

But the practice of scaling down causes a lot of frustration to those who want a decent-sized holding. Because the government is keen to encourage large numbers of investors you might find, in some cases, that people applying for large amounts, say, 5,000 shares, get none at all. So it doesn't make sense to be too greedy when applying for privatisation issues. On the other hand you should ask for more than you want since applications are often cut back owing to the numbers of people applying.

But be warned. If the issue proves less successful than you expect you could find you are given all the shares you asked for. If they don't open at a profit you could be facing a loss in early dealings if the shares are traded at below the issue price.

Theoretically you should know how many shares you have been given before dealing in the shares starts on the stockmarket. But with the big privatisations you may not actually receive your allotment letter in the post until several days after. But the basis of allotment will be announced officially a few days before dealings, enabling you to work out what you have received. In the case of a privatisation for instance it might be announced that everyone who subscribed for between 500 and 1,000 shares received 500 – there are endless permutations.

Sell or hold?

Shares should be regarded as investments. But the overwhelming success of the privatisations means that many people want to sell their shares immediately because they see a good quick profit. At around the time of a privatisation there will be plenty of institutions offering cut price selling services. Most stockbrokers will lump several small holdings of different family members into one – charging just one selling commission.

Stagging is the traditional term for investors who apply for new issues in the hope of a quick profit. There is nothing wrong with that – arguably it helps create a liquid market in the early days – but if the issue flops you will have to hold on to your shares or sell at a loss. It can be risky and you are not advised to borrow money to do it.

Sometimes, there is less opportunity for stagging, simply because there are fewer really inviting new issues where shares are available to the general public. Privatisations, apart from the straightforward offers for sale, are few and far between. Big institutional investors have used their muscle to persuade the City issuing houses that they should get their share of any decent issue regardless of what the public wants.

Many new issues are now done by way of a placing, with half of the shares on offer going to big investors and the other half being offered to the public. That cuts down the number of shares available to small investors – but it does ensure that the issue will not flop and makes it more certain of opening at a premium. Unfortunately the most exciting new issues may be done simply as a placing to friendly institutions and there may be no offer for sale at all to the public.

If you happen to be a regular client you might find some are offered to the private investors. And sometimes shares are offered to other stockbrokers and their clients too.

If there is a placing in a company that you particularly fancy ask your stockbroker or financial adviser about the possibility of getting some shares – but you will probably have to pay a commission when you buy.

Assessing new issues.

If you do spot an offer for sale you like the look of, the safest way of testing whether it is worth going for is to look at the press. Newspapers and investment magazines do get it wrong sometimes, but they usually have a pretty good idea of whether you are looking at a goer or a flop. From them you can glean the City gossip, what the all-important institutions think of it. New stockmarket companies can catch the imagination if they represent a new or fashionable sector. Lots of good publicity usually ensures a successful flotation.

As well as that, you should look carefully at the prospectus which will tell you about the company, the dividends, the profits, the trading record etc. Compare the price/earnings ratio and dividend yield with other quoted companies in the same line of business. The new issue should be valued a little lower than its more established rivals. And make sure you are comparing like with like. If similar companies are rated on the basis of profit forecasts rather than last year's results you must adjust to make a true comparison.

It is also worth looking to see who is sponsoring the issue – which merchant bank or stockbroker. A reputable name counts for a lot – as do earlier new issue successes.

And, unless you are looking at a privatisation, it pays to be cynical about an ordinary offer for sale these days. Placings to investing institutions have become so popular in the City that you have to ask yourself why is this company offering shares to the public – letting the small investor in – when it's cheaper and more convenient to just dish them out to the big boys? Perhaps it's because there are few takers among the professional investors – perhaps it's because the company genuinely wants a good spread of shareholders. Do your homework and proceed with caution.

14

Takeover bids, rights and scrip issues.

When a company finds itself on the receiving end of a takeover bid it means a nice bonus if you happen to be a shareholder.

To get you to accept the offer, the bidder will offer an amount in cash or shares, or a combination of the two, above the current stockmarket price.

A contested bid may prove a bonanza as the bidding company may have to increase its offer in the face of fierce resistance from the board or a counter bid from another predator.

Takeover activity tends to go in cycles – witness the explosion in activity in the 1980s when huge takeovers hit the headlines. When the stockmarket is going strong, companies on the prowl can use the enhanced value of their shares to make acquisitions. When the share prices are weak, takeovers become less popular.

Identifying bid targets.

But investors should keep an eye out for likely bid targets to add a bit of speculative spice to their share portfolio. Read the financial press – there are often bid rumours reported which may be worth investigating, and look for other signs.

These might include the acquisition of a large block of shares in a company by another group, which may herald the start of a takeover. Sometimes the stake is sold on. Sometimes the purchaser just sits there with it. But sometimes a bid does materialise – though you can never bank on it.

Companies held back by uninspired management may be a bid target. If a company seems to be lagging behind its sector rivals, find out why. Another company may well see an opportunity to make more money out of a basically sound business that is poorly managed.

Companies that are weighed down by loss-making divisions, heavy borrowings or over expansion are vulnerable to takeover. A predator may see a good financial opportunity in reorganising the business by cutting losses and selling off the profitable parts.

When a takeover bid is announced you do not have to do anything immediately. If it is opposed by the incumbent board you will receive masses of propaganda from both sides over the next few weeks. And you can be pretty certain that the first offer made will be increased. Even if the bid is agreed by both sides, there is always the chance of a higher counter offer from another company. Keep an eye on the market price of the shares – if it is higher than the value of the offer, it tells you that a better one is expected. Even if no rival bidder emerges, the predator often has to improve on the initial offer to secure acceptance from the big financial institutions. The only thing to worry about at this stage is the possibility of the bid being referred to the Monopolies and Mergers Commission which keeps an eye on takeovers and mergers. A reference usually kills the bid stone dead because it means months of investigation. If you think there is a strong chance of a referral you might want to sell your shares in the stockmarket while the going is good.

There are all kinds of City rules and regulations on takeovers, most of which need not concern shareholders. The official offer document you receive will set out the terms of the bid and the closing date for acceptance.

There is little point in accepting at once – though if you accept and the bidder is later forced to make a higher offer, you will get the higher offer in most circumstances, so you do not lose out. But while there is the chance of a rival bid there is nothing to be lost by waiting. At some point, however, you are going to have to make some decisions.

Decision time.

Not all bids succeed. Some companies have mounted successful campaigns to keep their independence in the face of a takeover attempt, getting the backing of loyal shareholders. What you decide is up to you. You must look at the detail of the offer. It may be all cash or all shares or a combination of both. Often there is an offer of shares with a cash alternative. You have to choose.

The value of any share offer to you depends on the market price and prospects of the bidding company – often its share price falls a little during the course of a bid. You have to consider whether you want shares in the company. The advantage of taking a share offer is that you are not liable for Capital Gains Tax when you swap. This is important if you have built up a sizable profit on your holding.

If you take a cash offer you will be liable for CGT. Much depends on the amount of profit and the way you use your annual CGT exemption. On the other hand, cash means certainty – you know exactly how much you are going to get. But before you accept a cash offer you should compare it with the value of your shares on the stockmarket. If they are higher, sell there instead.

Rights issues.

When a quoted company wants to raise money it can either borrow from the bank or ask its shareholders to put up the cash by buying more shares. The latter is obviously the cheapest option for the company. But a rights issue, as it is called, is rarely popular with shareholders who regard it as an occupational hazard of stockmarket investment.

But it is not necessarily all bad news. Rights issues can result in a substantial fall in company borrowings and interest which benefits profits and earnings. Rights issues can be a good way of financing expansion. Alternatively a rights issue may be a response to a crisis, launched as a last-ditch effort to save a company from going under. Whether you take up your rights to the shares or not may depend on what you feel about the company's prospects. You will be sent a document detailing the offer and telling you how the money will be used. You can find out what the market thinks about the rights issue by reading the press or asking your stockbroker.

You will be offered new shares in proportion to the amount you already have. So a rights issue may be one share for, say, every three or four or five you hold. The price of the new shares will be below the current market price – 20% is a rough average – to entice you to buy. But the announcement of the rights issue will have an immediate effect on the value of your existing holding. The share price may fall initially – by how much depends on the size and the terms of the issue. The adjusted price is called the ex-rights price.

But there is no reason why individual shareholders should buy new shares if they do not want to. If the company is basically sound the financial institutions will have them. But you have to face the fact that, at least for the moment, the value of your holding may well be less and the company's earnings will be diluted. Alternatively you may welcome an opportunity to add more shares to your holding without having to pay dealing costs or stamp duty.

Here are some points to watch. Some rights issues flop because the big financial institutions do not want them. If the price of the new shares is very near or above the price quoted on the stockmarket, something is wrong and you normally should not buy them. If you do not want the new shares, you may be able to sell your "nil paid rights" in the stockmarket for a handy profit. Ask your stockbroker – and find out first if it is worthwhile once you have paid his commission.

If you do nothing the company will eventually sell your nil paid rights for you and send you a cheque, if there is a profit in it.

Scrip issues.

Scrip, or capitalisation, issues are different from rights issues. You don't pay for the new shares, which is why they are sometimes known as bonus issues. But, as with rights issues, you get extra shares in proportion to the amount you already own – one for three, for example. The company merely increases its nominal capital and the market price of the shares adjusts to take account of the increased number of shares. Companies have scrip issues when they feel their share prices are getting too heavy.

Individual investors seem to like having scrip issues – they can sometimes perk up the market price a bit. But remember to mark the changed prices carefully in your records – a forgotten scrip issue can seriously muddle your calculations.

15

Your share portfolio.

There are theories galore about picking shares. Every expert has a system. It might be based on fundamental analysis, looking at charts, or sticking a pin in the prices pages of the *Financial Times*. But running a successful share portfolio is not just about picking whizz-bang winners. It's about organising your investments to help you achieve your personal financial objectives.

- What kind of return do you want?
- How much risk can your nerves stand?
- Do you need income now?
- Or are you investing for a nest egg in the future?

Everyone has different requirements. But there are several broad categories that cover most stockmarket investors. And the way you handle your portfolio depends on how you see yourself.

- *You earn a comfortable income with a pension but you want to build up some capital. You don't have a lot of time to devote to the stockmarket and you don't like taking big risks.*

You need a share portfolio to give you long-term capital appreciation and reasonable security. A mixture of Blue Chip and growth shares would be appropriate plus some unit and/or investment trusts.

Your share portfolio will not be particularly active. But you need to make sure that you are beating inflation and at least doing as well, if not better, than the stockmarket as a whole.

- *You are nearing or in retirement and you want to secure a high-income return from your investments.*

You need to put a proportion of your capital in gilts and other fixed-interest investments when interest rates are high – timing this well is very important. Your share portfolio should include higher-yielding shares and Blue Chip companies. Even if income is your chief objective your equity portfolio will be the main way to protect your capital from inflation – and to supplement your income by taking some profits when interest rates are low. You should make use of personal equity plans – as well as allowing capital gains free of tax, the income from them is tax-free, unlike your pension.

- *You really enjoy playing the stockmarket and are prepared to spend time studying it. Even if you want to get a significant income out of your portfolio you may well choose to do it by investing for capital growth and taking profits on a regular basis.*

Your share portfolio should reflect your active interest. You might opt for a selection of growth stocks plus special riskier situations – penny shares, prospective bid candidates, recovery stocks and so on. But be sure that you have the time and interest to keep a careful eye on them day to day. And only speculate with money you can afford to lose.

Whatever kind of investor you feel you are there are some general rules of portfolio management that apply to all.

Spread the risks.

You need to have enough different shares to give yourself a reasonable spread of investments. Even if you are going entirely for Blue Chips you must spread the risk – even the most solid companies can hit a bad patch. Aim to hold a handful of different shares.

You should invest in several sectors rather than concentrating on just one. This doesn't mean that you shouldn't have more invested in, say, retailing if you think there is a recovery in consumer spending on the horizon. Just do not put all your eggs in the same basket.

Don't, on the other hand, have too many shares. It will be a headache keeping track of them all. How many different shares you hold depends partly on the amount of money you have to invest. Dealing in very small quantities can be expensive because of minimum commission rates. Half a dozen to a dozen shares is a rough guideline for most private investors. Ideally, aim for at least £1,000 in each share, or certainly not less than £500.

Check your portfolio.

Get in the habit of checking the progress of your investments on a regular basis – noting movements in prices daily, weekly or monthly. It will give you some feel for the way certain shares or sectors react to general movements or events. It will show you which shares are earning their keep and which are lagging behind. And shares which move against the trend – fall when the market rises, or rise when it falls – are giving you a buy or sell sign well worth heeding.

When to sell.

Selling shares well is almost more important than choosing which ones to buy. Never mind paper profits. The only ones which matter are the ones you take, the money you put in the bank.

The basic rule is to let profits run, and to cut losses quickly. In practice, it seems, private investors often do exactly the opposite. It is easy to persuade yourself that duds need a little more time, and will come right. And if you take that profit on a winner, you can afford to hang on to the loser a little longer.

Do not do it. In practice, someone in the market always knows more than you. Listen to what the share price is telling you. A little dip may not matter. But a consistent fall tells you that other people are selling. They probably have a good reason for it. Heed the message. You should sell, too.

Stop-loss system.

Some people swear by a stop-loss system. When you buy a share you make a mental note to sell should the price fall by, say, 20%. It takes discipline to do it, and sometimes losers bounce back, and you end up selling a good share too soon. But, in general, a stop-loss system is sensible. It means you never lose more than about 20%, plus dealings costs, on any one share.

Running your profits.

If you pick a winner, stay with it while it keeps going up. Others are buying it because they think it is good. Perhaps they know more than you. Once shares start moving, they tend to develop a momentum. Success generates success. Fast risers attract attention, and more buyers come in.

You can use a stop-loss system with winners too. Trail the stop loss level up behind the share price as it rises. If it slips more than, say, 20% from the peak, take the profits. You never get out at the top that way – only luck can ensure you do that – but you never let big profits slip completely away.

Others advocate selling half of your holding in any share when it doubles, so that the shares you keep have effectively cost you nothing. That works for some – but it takes skill and good fortune to buy a winner. It seems a shame to cut half of your possible gain just as it might really be getting going.

It is important to have a system, and impose self discipline when it comes to selling shares. Otherwise you will let your portfolio drift, and find yourself holding the duds and selling the good shares.

Timing.

You should also try to remember there are times – sometimes years – when it makes less sense to be in the share market. You do not have to be an economic genius to sense when things are getting tougher. The stockmarket is usually among the first indicators. When interest rates are rising, and perhaps the pound is under pressure, you know life is going to become more difficult for companies. Unless you are prepared to see your portfolio fall sharply for a long while before it recovers, you should seriously consider reducing your share portfolio. Put the money in a bank account, or a building society for a while.

Equally, of course, there will be times when it is plainly better to be in the market. If all the pointers suggest we are coming out of recession, share prices will be perking up. That is the time to think about reinvesting, switching some of your money from cash holdings into shares. Flexibility is one major advantage that the private investor has over the big financial institutions. Profit from it.

16

Investor protection.

The single most important phrase for any investor to understand is "Caveat Emptor" - "Buyer Beware". No one cares, or *can* care, quite as much about what happens to your hard-won cash as you do. This is not a cynical point of view. It is a statement of fact. In many ways, it is a reason for writing this book – a simple practical guide to the investment world that, hopefully, explains the basics.

member firm and a customer. The SROs are:

- The Securities and Futures Authority (SFA), which covers stockbrokers.
- The Life Assurance and Unit Trust Regulatory Organisation (LAUTRO), which covers life insurance and unit trust companies.
- The Investment Management Regulatory Organisation (IMRO), which covers investment managers.
- The Financial Intermediaries Managers and Brokers Regulatory Association (FIMBRA), which covers financial advisers.

In addition, there are nine recognised professional bodies (RPBs) covering solicitors, chartered accountants, insurance brokers, and actuaries who give personal finance advice.

There are, however, plans to simplify things by establishing the Personal Investment Authority (PIA) which will cover most forms of individual investment. Meanwhile, the crucial point is to check that any firm or individual you deal with is properly authorised. Otherwise you will not be legally protected in the event of things going wrong. The quickest way to do this is to contact SIB's central register by phoning 071-929 3652. You can check basic information on particular firms and individuals with them, free of charge.

Investors' compensation scheme.

However careful you are, things can go wrong. Investment firms can go bust, mishandle clients' money or give negligent advice that results in loss. If any of these things happen, you may have a claim for compensation under the Financial Services Act, provided the firm you dealt with was authorised. Individuals can claim for a maximum amount of £50,000. If your claim is successful you will receive a maximum of £48,000 – the first £30,000 in full plus 90% of the next £20,000. It is important to understand the limitations of the compensation scheme – and the fact that it does not cover investment losses due to a fall in the stockmarket.

SIB produces a number of free brochures explaining the system of investor protection. You can obtain these by writing to:

Securities and Investments Board
Gavrelle House
2-14 Bunhill Row
London EC1Y 8RA
071-638 1240

The Securities Institute.

The Securities Institute was founded in March 1992 as an independent professional body for those working in the investment business. It now has more than 8,000 Members and Associates of whom 2,500 offer services to private individuals. A Member of the Securities Institute - MSI - is qualified to give investment advice. Members must keep to an ethical code which includes high professional and technical standards following the spirit, as well as the letter of the law, and the avoidance of self-interest where it could conflict with the interests of clients. For further information, contact:

The Securities Institute
Centurion House
24 Monument Street
London EC3R 8AJ
071-626 3191

17

The ProShare Association.

Over the last few years millions of investors have been introduced to the stockmarket through the government's privatisation programme. People who had never owned a share before found it was easy, inexpensive – and profitable – to invest as the huge formerly State-owned utilities like British Telecom and the gas and electricity industries were transformed into major commercial organisations. But the privatisation programme was only the first step in the development of a shareholder culture which encourages private individuals to invest in the stockmarket.

ProShare is an organisation that works to achieve that goal. It believes that both individuals and the economy will benefit from the spread of share ownership, which brings together the interests of investors, employees and management in a common purpose. Investing in shares is the most direct way of taking a stake in the economy.

Despite the welcome increase in the number of individual shareholders, the stockmarket still remains dominated by the financial institutions, and only some 200,000 of those first time privatisation investors have gone on to buy shares in other stockmarket companies. As yet individual stockmarket investment plays far too small a role in our financial structure despite the growth of collective investments such as unit trusts. But as we approach the millennium it is clear that private individuals will be expected to shoulder much more responsibility for their financial futures – and stockmarket investment is a vital part of that process.

There is already much alarm about the impact of a larger ageing population on the economy – but the fact is that few of us can rely on pensions, State or private, to maintain our standard of living after retirement. Saving and investing is essential.

ProShare was launched in February 1992 with the backing of all major political parties and funding from the London Stock Exchange, the government and a large number of commercial organisations. Its purpose is to increase share ownership by private individuals and employees. A crucial part of its programme is The ProShare Association which is committed to helping more people invest in the stockmarket and supporting the cause of the private shareholder.

To an outsider the stockmarket may look a baffling and rather frightening place. Where do you go for help and advice? What does all the jargon mean? How can the private investor ever keep up with the professionals? The mystique surrounding the stockmarket is one of the main reasons why so few of those who bought privatisation shares have gone on to invest in others.

One of the main challenges for ProShare, then, has been to ensure that potential and existing shareholders have access to unbiased information and advice about the stockmarket. ProShare does that through an extensive education programme and the production of user-friendly guidance on investment. This book, for instance, aims to help the first-time stockmarket investor while other ProShare publications cater for the more experienced. ProShare helps companies who want to establish employee shareholder schemes and has launched a service for investment clubs.

The ProShare Association is designed to help the private individual investor. Annual membership costs £30.

Members receive a monthly newsletter, full of stimulating stockmarket news and views which provides the opportunity to take part in an investor programme of company visits and seminars. You will also get *ProShare's Guide to Information Sources* which gives an at-a-glance assessment of the key sources of information for private investors. Members also receive a portfolio management system to help keep you up to date with your investments, and discounts on a range of related products and services.

For further information on how to join The ProShare Association telephone 071-971 0061 (24 hours) or write to:

The ProShare Association
Freepost KE 8391
London
EC2B 2LD

18

Investment clubs.

Investing in the stockmarket is not just a way of building up capital or saving for your old age. As any keen private investor will tell you, following the stockmarket is a fascinating business. Picking your shares, watching what happens to them, weighing up the economic news, learning to sniff out opportunities, looking out for problems, all these elements mean investors find the stockmarket a stimulating hobby. It can be made even more exciting when they can share their interest with others through an investment club.

Investment clubs are not a new idea. There are hundreds of them up and down the country, thousands in other countries like the USA and France where investors have found that clubbing together to invest in the stockmarket is profitable and fun.

ProShare believes that investment clubs are one of the most important ways of encouraging individuals to invest in the stockmarket. There are already many investment clubs in the UK and ProShare is actively promoting the formation of many more. ProShare has relaunched the National Association of Investment Clubs, founded in the 1950s, as ProShare Investment Clubs Ltd (PIC), producing a detailed guide to setting up and running an investment club. If you are the sort of person who enjoys swapping ideas and knowledge you should consider starting onc of your own with like-minded friends.

There are a host of advantages in pooling your stockmarket investments in this way.

It can be expensive running your own portfolio, particularly if you only have a modest sum to invest. As we have seen, successful investment involves spreading the risk through buying a number of different shares in a variety of sectors. You may be able to achieve this better, at lower cost, by pooling your resources through an investment club. It's like having your own unit trust. And with more money to invest a club may find it easier to get good advice from the professionals.

Doing your research is a crucial part of successful stockmarket investment. But it is time consuming. Club members can agree to look at different companies and sectors – maybe specialising in industries where they have particular knowledge or contacts. An investment club is the ideal forum for debating investment ideas. Everyone has their own point of view – discussion is a good way to learn more. Many clubs invite guest speakers to talk about aspects of investment. If you're an absolute beginner you will learn from other members. If you are an experienced stockmarket investor it's an opportunity to get together with others who share the same interests.

Members agree how much money each should put in the "pot" – usually an initial amount, then a set sum each month. So joining an investment club means that you are setting aside a regular sum for your stockmarket investment which is a good savings discipline.

The most successful investment clubs operate on the basis of co-operation between friends who enjoy meeting each other. You can have your monthly meetings anywhere – at members' houses or in the pub. It should be a sociable event.

The laws relating to partnerships mean you can't have more than 20 members in an investment club. Between ten and 15 is a sensible number to aim for. There will be enough of you to get the benefits of "collective" investment but not too many to spoil the club atmosphere or make decision making difficult.

How an investment club works.

There are no hard and fast rules about how to organise your investment club, but ProShare has some recommendations on the best way forward. Most important is establishing how the members' investments will be accounted for so that everyone knows how well they are doing.

Typically the members will put in a lump sum to start with – £50 or £100 or even more depending how quickly you want to start investing. Then the members will fix the regular monthly payment – £15, £20 or more, that they will all make. It's important that everyone is comfortable with the amount chosen. You will probably be wise to wait a couple of months before investing any money – until you have built up a reasonable sum – say £500 minimum. By then you will be really keen to get going with your ideas.

There are different ways of running the fund. ProShare favours the unit valuation system – one of the simplest methods of monitoring the value of members' investments.

At the beginning, each £1 contributed gives members one unit. To work out the value of the units once the fund starts investing, you divide the number of units into the value of the club's assets. Those assets will be cash subscribed, plus the market value of all investments made, minus dealing costs and any other expenses. The fund should be revalued each month. The new unit value is used to calculate the number of units to be purchased with each month's cash subscriptions. Within this framework it is possible for new members to join and for others to buy extra units or sell part of their holding if necessary.

Starting an investment club requires careful preparatory work. Getting founding members together is only the first stage. You must then decide who is to chair meetings, who is to look after the administration, where the money will be held, who will have access to it, and what kind of stockmarket dealing or advice service you require.

There may be trustees to be appointed (no one has yet run off with investment club money but security is obviously crucial), tax implications to be studied and accounting methods to be decided on.

You may find all this a little daunting – which is one reason why ProShare has developed a package of information and support systems to help you and your friends get an investment club up and running.

You don't have to join PIC. But the annual £50 subscription will prove an excellent investment. You will receive the *ProShare Investment Clubs Manual* – a unique step by step guide that explains every aspect of setting up an investment club. It gives expert advice on everything from computer software to make administration easier to dealing with a stockbroker.

You will receive each month *The ProShare Bulletin* to keep you up to date with the stockmarket and the *ProShare Guide to Information Sources* – a directory of investment advice services. You will have access to a telephone helpline and special offers and discounts on some ProShare publications.

For a brochure explaining how to obtain the PIC manual and the benefits of membership, please telephone freephone 0800-556622, or write to:

ProShare Investment Clubs
Library Chambers
13 & 14 Basinghall St
London EC2V 5BQ.

APPENDIX

A to Z of investment.

A **ALLOTMENT LETTER.** If you apply for a privatisation or new issue this tells you how many shares you have been given.

ASSETS are what a company owns – land, machinery, stocks, cash and investments. Deduct liabilities like loans and creditors and you get NET ASSET VALUE – what the company might be worth if it were wound up.

AT BEST is an instruction to your stockbroker to buy or sell shares for the best price available.

B **BID PRICE.** The price at which you sell shares.

BLUE CHIP. A big, well-known company whose shares are considered low risk.

C **CONVERTIBLE LOAN STOCKS** pay fixed interest but can be converted into shares at a given price at set times.

CREST is a proposed system for electronic transfer of shares. But private investors will still be able to obtain actual share certificates.

CUM. If a share is quoted CUM dividend or CUM rights issue it means that it still bears the entitlement and this is reflected in the price.

D **DEPRECIATION** is the financial equivalent of wear and tear. Businesses deduct a certain amount from profits to reflect the decline in value of plant and machinery.

DISCRETIONARY ACCOUNT. Your stockbroker or financial adviser can make investment decisions without necessarily consulting you.

E **EQUITIES** is another term for ordinary shares.

EX. A share price may be quoted as EX dividend or EX rights. It means the buyer will not have entitlement to the recent dividend payment or rights issue.

F **FLAT YIELD.** The income return on a fixed-interest investment at current price.

FLOTATION. When a company's shares are brought to the stockmarket and quoted for the first time.

G **GEARING.** Company borrowing as a proportion of shareholders' funds. A HIGHLY GEARED company is a riskier investment but when times are good earnings grow faster.

GROSS describes the value before deductions. An investment may be described as yielding 10% gross – that means before deduction of income tax.

H **HEDGE.** An investment that gives protection – against inflation, for instance, or currency risks.

I **INDEX-LINKED** means the return from an investment will reflect the official trend in price inflation.

INSIDER DEALING. If directors, stockbrokers, others close to the company or members of the public deal in its shares on the basis of confidential information they are guilty of a criminal offence.

ISSUE PRICE. Price at which shares are first offered to investors when a company floats on the stockmarket.

J **JOBBERS** were part of the old Stock Exchange system – stockbrokers bought and sold shares through them. Now prices are made by MARKET MAKERS.

K **KRUGERRANDS** are South African coins containing 1oz of gold, a popular way for small investors to speculate in the gold price.

L **LONG.** If an investor is LONG of a share it means he has bought a lot of it.

LONGS. Market term for government stocks (gilts) that have over 15 years to go until they are due to be repaid.

M **MEDIUMS.** Market term for gilts (government securities) that have between five and 15 years to go before repayment.

MIDDLE MARKET PRICE. Halfway between the buying and selling prices of a share. Most newspapers use the MIDDLE PRICE in their daily stockmarket lists for convenience.

N **NET** means after deductions. A NET return on an investment describes its value after tax has been deducted.

NOMINAL VALUE means the face or par value of shares or other investments as opposed to the MARKET VALUE – what you can buy or sell at now.

O **OFFER PRICE.** Price at which you buy a share.

OVERSUBSCRIBED is when a new issue attracts more applications than there are shares available.

P **PREFERENCE SHARES** rank before ordinary shares for dividend payments, and in the event of a company being wound up preference shares must be repaid before equity holders get anything. Preference shares offer a fixed return – the dividends on ordinary shares go up and down depending on profits.

PREMIUM. Upward difference between issue price of a share or other investment and its market value.

Q **QUOTE.** The current price for buying and selling a share offered by a market maker.

R **REVERSE YIELD GAP.** The difference between the return on shares and the return on fixed interest investments. Shares used to yield more than gilts because they were considered riskier investments. Inflation has reversed that assumption – fixed-interest investments now yield more than equities.

ROLLING SETTLEMENT means that shares have to be paid for within a certain number of days following each transaction. This will replace the traditional Stock Exchange ACCOUNT system.

S **SETTLEMENT DAY** is the date when Stock Exchange transactions must be paid for or settled.

SHORTS. Market term for gilts (government securities) that have less than five years to go before repayment.

STOCKBROKER. Someone who buys and sells shares and other Stock Exchange securities on behalf of clients.

SUSPENSION. Trading in a share can be halted by the Stock Exchange – a company might ask for a temporary suspension of dealings – if a takeover bid is under discussion for instance. Sometimes a suspension means bad news is on the way.

T **TENDER.** A way of auctioning shares or gilt-edged securities to the highest bidders. A guide is announced – then investors have to make up their own minds how much to offer for the amount of stock they want.

TOUCH. Competing market makers quote slightly different prices for a share. The TOUCH is the difference between the best bid price and the lowest offer price.

U **UNDATED SECURITIES** have no repayment date. War Loan is one example.

W **WORKING CAPITAL** is the cash needed to finance the everyday running of a business such as the payment of salaries and the purchase of raw materials. Most companies that go bust do so because a shortage of working capital leads to a CASH FLOW CRISIS.

Y **YIELD** is the annual rate you get on an investment through payment of dividends or interest.

Z **ZERO-COUPON BONDS** do not pay interest. They are issued at a deep discount to the redemption price so that the investor receives the return in the form of capital gain rather than income.

INDEX